THE ART OF
SCOTTISH
GOLF

THE ART OF SCOTTISH GOLF

Where it all began…

MARTIN DEMPSTER

Black&White

Black&White

First published in the UK in 2024 by
Black & White Publishing Ltd
Nautical House, 104 Commercial Street, Edinburgh, EH6 6NF

A division of Bonnier Books UK
4th Floor, Victoria House, Bloomsbury Square, London, WC1B 4DA
Owned by Bonnier Books
Sveavägen 56, Stockholm, Sweden

A CIP catalogue record for this book is available from the British Library.

ISBN: 978 1 78530 710 2

1 3 5 7 9 10 8 6 4 2

Layout by creativelink.tv
Printed and bound in Lithuania

www.blackandwhitepublishing.com

For Carol, Amy and Katie -
my foundation, inspiration and motivation

Dunbar Golf Club.

CONTENTS

1

GOLF IS SCOTLAND'S NATIONAL SPORT

The 18th hole on the Old Course and the R&A Clubhouse.

The iconic Swilcan Bridge on the Old Course at St Andrews.

Forget football. Forget rugby. In fact, forget any other sport you can come up with. Because golf is what most people around the world think of when Scotland is mentioned in a sporting capacity. Yes, Andy Murray may have been the country's leading light in sport for the last decade or so through making his mark in tennis at a time when he was up against the likes of Roger Federer, Rafa Nadal and Novak Djokovic. Yes, the country also produced an Olympic great in Chris Hoy, who pedalled his way to six gold and one silver medal in the biggest sporting event

of them all. And, yes, Scottish teams are renowned for playing with pride and passion on some of the biggest stages in football and rugby.

It's golf, though, that really resonates around the globe when Scotland is mentioned in a sporting sense – and rightly so. Its history: the sport originated from a game played on the east coast of the country in the 16th century and quickly spread throughout Europe. Its pioneers: Scots have travelled far and wide to make their mark in the game. Its courses: links in particular but also some inland gems, providing a menu that is widely regarded as second to none. Its people: the country being awash with individuals who not only love golf themselves but go out of their way in many different capacities to help visitors from all over the world fully appreciate why Scotland is the "Home of Golf".

"I think what makes golf special in Scotland is a community aspect," says Stephen Gallacher, who followed in the footsteps of his uncle Bernard Gallacher, by not only falling in love with the game but also matching his feats in becoming a winner in the professionals ranks and playing in the Ryder Cup, the sport's biggest event in terms of audience numbers. "In Bathgate, where I cut my golfing teeth, there's a club in the middle of the town. In St Andrews, people are allowed to walk on the Old Course on a Sunday when, unlike every other course in the country, it's closed to golfers."

St Nicholas Golf Course, Prestwick.

Leith Links in Edinburgh, where the game officially became a sport through the forming of the Gentlemen Golfers of Leith Club in 1744, will forever be synonymous with golf in Scotland; as will venues like Prestwick, where The Open, the sport's "original championship", was first played in 1860 and staged for 11 consecutive years before starting to move around the country, and Musselburgh, where the course is now encircled by a horse-racing track. Other towns such as North Berwick, Carnoustie, Nairn and Troon have all been put on the map thanks to golf, but, with all due respect to everywhere else, it's St Andrews that sets pulses racing and not just for golfers. Yes, of course, the chance to enjoy a hit on the Old Course is on the bucket list of every single person who plays the game, but a photo opportunity with it in the background is every bit as special to non-golfers as they are dropped off by their tourist buses behind the clubhouse of the Royal & Ancient Golf Club just as they are at Edinburgh Castle, for example, or at numerous other stunning and famous locations around the country.

Players competing in the Leith Rules Golf Society Hickory Open in July 2022. Edinburgh City Council give LRGS permission to hold a golf week on Leith Links and for them the week serves both as a celebration and a reminder of Leith's golfing heritage. All the games are played with hickory clubs and sand is used to tee the ball up, as was the custom in the past.

Leith Links, Edinburgh.

Retail store of golf club manufacturer St Andrews Golf Company, "oldest golf club manufacturer in the world". St Andrews, Fife.

I live in the Kingdom of Fife, yet will never tire of making an hour-long journey to St Andrews; my favourite route being through Leven and Lundin Links before taking the A915 in Upper Largo that climbs over the hill before St Andrews, with the Tay Estuary and Angus coast as a stunning backdrop, soon appears in front of your eyes. It's equally special making the journey on the A917 from Crail as the East Sands come into view as you head down towards the town from Kinkell Braes. Even long-time residents of the Auld Grey Toun never forget about it as somewhere that William and Kate – now the Prince and Princess of Wales – may have brought to the attention of a younger audience through meeting in one of the local coffee shops when they were both studying at the University of St Andrews, but the town reeks golf at almost every corner.

"I'm never bored walking the streets of St Andrews and never will be as the human mosaic changes all the time," declares David Scott, who grew up in the town and, through golf, has become a well-kent face in the game, having been handed the honour of becoming the captain of the Professional Golfers' Association (PGA), one of the sport's biggest and most-respected bodies, in 2025. "It just oozes history. St Andrews University has been here for even longer than the Old Course and, when walking

Prince William and Kate Middleton met when they were both studying at the University of St Andrews.

through the town, as I do on a regular basis, I never take for granted just how lucky I am to be in such a wonderful town with such an incredible golfing heritage that, frankly, is unparalleled. So many incredible people have walked the same hallowed ground – Old Tom Morris and his son, Young Tom, Bobby Jones, Jack Nicklaus, Seve Ballesteros, Tiger Woods and our own Sandy Lyle. Then there's University alumni, the Prince and Princess of Wales, as well as former presidents of the United States, and also countless celebrities flying into Leuchars on private jets to play in the Alfred Dunhill Links Championship [an event on the DP World Tour staged at St Andrews, Carnoustie and Kingsbarns Links]."

At the last official count, a total of 567 clubs were affiliated with Scottish Golf, the game's governing body in Scotland. The best-known, of course, are those that regularly stage big championships, and no championships come bigger in the United Kingdom and Ireland than The Open. With thirty now to its name, St Andrews has hosted what is now the Claret Jug event – a Challenge Belt, which was made from red leather and worth £25, was the winner's prize in its formative years – more than any other course, with Muirfield (16), Royal Troon (10) and Carnoustie (8) being the other Scottish courses currently on the R&A's list of venues for its marquee men's event. Turnberry, where it has been staged on four occasions, most recently in 2009, has not been under consideration since it was bought by Donald Trump in 2014. The AIG Women's Open, also now run by the R&A, has been staged at both Royal Troon and Muirfield, home of the Honourable Company of Edinburgh Golfers, as well as Carnoustie and Turnberry in recent years, after already breaking new ground before that at St Andrews, where it was held for a third time in 2024.

> I think what makes golf special in Scotland is a community aspect.

STEPHEN GALLACHER

Its beauty, though, in a golfing sense, is that the country is awash with top-class courses, many of which may never have necessarily received exposure by hosting either professional or amateur tournaments but, nonetheless, are on must-play lists for the tens of thousands of golf-mad visitors who flock to Scotland on an annual basis. Knowing they are in for a treat no matter what a particular day may serve up either on the weather front or in terms of a personal performance. Whether it's on the coast or deep into the heart of one of the most beautiful countries in the world, there's something almost therapeutic about walking the fairways in the land that spawned the great game.

"The fact it is the Home of Golf makes it special," says Richie Ramsay, who cut his teeth in the game in Aberdeen and became the first British golfer in more than a century to win the US Amateur Championship before becoming a multiple title holder in the professional game. "Just the way golf weaves itself through the fabric of society in Scotland. It's the origins of the game, the way the courses have been laid out and, in lots of cases, the way they are built into the towns. Also when you see people walking down the streets with their golf clubs. It's almost like the gift we've given the world when you look and see how it's spread through other countries. I also like the fact it's generally a sport people look up to and admire."

I've often found myself laughing as my American friends in particular seem to think us Scots get into golf through falling straight out of the womb on to the first tee. The fact of the matter is that, in the vast majority of cases at least, it's in the family. In my instance, it was through my dad, who introduced me to the game at Eyemouth on the Berwickshire coast. I still remember getting my first set of clubs as a Christmas present one year and, needless to say, they were duly broken in before sitting down with the rest of the family for our festive feast.

Dumbarnie Links in Fife staged the Trust Golf Women's Scottish Open in 2021.

I live in the Kingdom of Fife, yet will never tire of making an hour-long journey to St Andrews.

I was instantly hooked and spent most days of the summer holidays playing what was then a nine-hole course. Though large chunks of these days, I have to confess, were spent clambering down into the deep gullies to retrieve golf balls that had ended up there due to wayward shots.

Fifty years on, I may not necessarily have improved, but there's nothing that beats spending a few hours out in the Scottish air with some buddies and indulging in a bit of banter, something that Scots are renowned for, and few places are better for than out in the open on a golf course. Most of my life skills were learned from being around my dad and his mates, either playing golf or spending an hour or so afterwards with them in the clubhouse at Dunbar. Thanks to the likes of first-class junior foundations now being operated by Stephen Gallacher in and around Edinburgh, and Paul Lawrie in the northeast, that culture remains an important role that golf can play when it comes to society in general.

Both Gallacher and Lawrie, who enjoyed a day to savour as he was crowned as Open champion at Carnoustie, an hour or so from his home city of Aberdeen, in 1999, have become fantastic ambassadors for the Scottish game. As has Catriona Matthew, another major winner and a Solheim Cup legend after playing nine times in the women's equivalent of the Ryder Cup. She then created history as the first European captain to record back-to-back wins over the Americans, the first of those also happening to come on home soil in a dramatic 2019 encounter at Gleneagles. That came five years after Irishman Paul McGinley, who was up against one of the legends of the game in Tom Watson, led Europe to victory in the Ryder Cup, with both those events showcasing Scotland at its finest as a country steeped in golf.

Winning European captain Catriona Matthew holds aloft the Solheim Cup at Gleneagles in 2019.

GROWING THE GAME

The sport of golf in general has long been regarded as being on the stuffy side. Slowly but surely, though, it is being modernised and rightly so. After 260 years as a male bastion, the Royal & Ancient Golf Club of St Andrews opened its doors to female members in 2014, a significant moment in the game's history. A whole host of other clubs, including the Honourable Company of Edinburgh Golfers, Royal Troon, the Royal Burgess Golfing Society and Bruntsfield Links Golfing Society, all subsequently followed the R&A's lead and took the same step. Lots of clubs around the country have also seen women serve as club captains in the past decade, with Scottish Golf having been formed through an amalgamation of the Scottish Ladies Golfing Association and Scottish Golf Union in 2015.

Even in Scotland, however, the game can have its problems and there have been several club closures over the years. Brunston Castle in Ayrshire, for example, as well as Whitekirk in East Lothian and both Lothianburn and Torphin Hill on the outskirts of Edinburgh are no longer open. If it hadn't been for golf enjoying a massive participation boom as it was one of the few sports to be permitted as the country dealt with the Covid-19 pandemic, more doors would probably have closed. The constant threat of closure

> "I'm never bored walking the streets of St Andrews and never will be as the human mosaic changes all the time."
>
> DAVID SCOTT

still hangs over a few courses, but some clubs have adapted to a world where the traditional golf club model doesn't necessarily fit all.

Take Callander, for instance. The Trossachs club had endured a difficult decade due to falling member and visitor numbers before a decision to make it a community-focused, family-friendly club led to a turnaround in its fortunes. A new purpose-built clubhouse – named Old Tom's Rest in honour of Old Tom Morris, who designed the course – was opened in 2013 and, in under 12 months, a target of attracting a hundred new members was hit. In short, its future has been secured and, as a result, it has now become a golfing hub for the town.

Clubhouse at Callander Golf Club.

Callander Golf Club.

Family golf centres, including one owned and operated by Lawrie on the outskirts of Aberdeen and others like Wellsgreen in Fife and Kingsfield in West Lothian, have done a splendid job of showing that venues with first-class practice facilities and nine-hole courses – and don't forget nice cafés or restaurants – have a part to play in the ongoing battle to "grow the game".

Martin Slumbers spotted this during his term as CEO of the R&A, the game's governing body outside of the United States which is based in St Andrews. Freely admitting he'd used that sort of facility as his template, he was the driving force behind Golf It!, a fantastic new community venue that opened on the outskirts of Glasgow in 2023 and, based on how well it has already been received, is set to achieve an ultimate target of "revolutionising the sport" and "making it more accessible and inclusive".

Slumbers says: "I believe that Golf It! is a compelling model that we can take elsewhere to show the golf and leisure industry that this kind of package with golf at its heart can be commercially successful but, just as importantly, can create pathways into the game for many more players from all ages and backgrounds."

That, in a short form, is why golf in Scotland is so important, both to those who are lucky enough to live in our great wee country and also to those who come here via plane, train, boat, car, bus or bicycle even – with their golf clubs in tow! But it's worth diving deeper into why that is the case as we celebrate one of Scotland's greatest exports.

The R&A's Golf It! facility in Glasgow opened in 2023.

Forget football. Forget rugby.
In fact, forget any other sport
you can come up with.

2

GOLF IS PLAYED FROM CRADLE TO GRAVE

6th hole Carnoustie Championship Course.

Spend any reasonable amount of time in a golf environment in Scotland and you are likely to hear the phrase "from cradle to grave". It's a well-coined phrase in relation to golf in our wee country and not just something that people pluck out of the air to give the game a sort of Hollywood-style spin. All around the country, people take up the game as whippersnappers and are still swinging a golf club as pensioners. "Golf is one of the few sports that can be played from cradle to grave," observes Robbie Clyde, chief executive officer of Scottish Golf, the game's governing body in its birthplace.

The majority of Scots are hooked for life once they've been introduced to the game at an early age, most likely by a parent or through a family connection. Others may drift away from the sport in their twenties before returning to the fairways later in life as they, in turn, introduce a new generation to the game. Visit most clubs and, at some point, there's a good chance you'll come across three generations out having fun together and that's one of golf's great beauties.

"Oh, it's given me a huge amount," says Solheim Cup legend Catriona Matthew, as she reflects on what the game has meant to her since cutting her teeth in North Berwick, where she has lived all her life and now resides close to the 18th tee on the West Links in the East Lothian town. "Obviously I love the game and it was a great family game for us and still is. In that respect, it was good that we could do something as a family and now my youngest daughter, Sophie, is getting into the game too. I love that part of the game. That you can play with anyone and it doesn't matter how good or bad they are at it or what age they are. I think that's what I love most about golf – that and, of course, the friendships. Now that I'm not playing on tour anymore, I'm back playing with people I grew up playing with or played with in Scottish teams back in the day. The game has obviously given me a living as well. I've travelled the world with my husband

Graeme, so it has given me a huge amount. It's been my whole life, really."

Paul Lawrie, another Scottish major winner, made more than 600 appearances on the DP World Tour, and is still going strong on the over-50s Legends Tour. Yet nothing comes close to the genuine pleasure he gets from being out on a course in the Aberdeen area with his two golf-mad sons, Craig and Michael, as well as his nephew, Sean. "It's still the best time I have playing golf – you cannot beat it," he says. "It doesn't matter how I play or what I shoot. Playing with them, it's just a fantastic feeling." In truth, he doesn't like losing to them, but that's down to the competitive streak that turned him from a five-handicapper when he became a professional into a top player.

Paul Lawrie and his son Craig.

Catriona Matthew, husband Graeme, and daughters Katie and Sophie

Another Aberdonian, Richie Ramsay, also cherishes his family memories out on the golf course. "I would play the nine-holer at Hazlehead when I was growing up with my grandfather, who would take me and my brother to play," he says in sharing his most special moment playing the game on Scottish soil. "I'd try like a bear to beat my brother even though he was four years older than me and would continually outdrive me. That still holds strong to this day. I've still got those memories ingrained in my head, even though it was 30 years ago."

Hazlehead Park in Aberdeen.

A FAR-REACHING SPORT

At the most recent count, a total of 567 clubs were affiliated to Scottish Golf, meaning members of those individual clubs paid a fee as part of their annual subscription that goes towards helping the governing body with its operational costs. In the figures returned by clubs for 2023, the total number of playing members in the country was 210,012. Breaking that down, the total number of men was 166,363 compared to 22,289 women. The figures for boys and girls were 17,620 and 3,740 respectively. Encouragingly, 2023 produced a seven per cent increase in junior membership, with 45 clubs doubling their junior numbers. In addition to all of that, the latest figures from a report by the Professional Golfers' Association suggested that in Scotland there are an additional 500,000 casual golfers – i.e. not club members – playing as visitors, not just at courses but also at driving ranges, adventure golf, pitch and putt and so on.

"The importance of golf to Scotland is broad and multi-faceted," says Clyde, who spent 30 years working in the private and public sectors across sports, major events, tourism, international trade and manufacturing before taking up the reins at Scottish Golf, which was created through an amalgamation between

Scottish Golf CEO Robbie Clyde spent 30 years working in the private and public sector.

Scottish Golf and the Scottish Ladies Golf in 2015. "The contribution of the sport to the nation's wider economy is estimated to be over £1 billion, and golf tourism alone contributes around £300 million per annum.

"Golf has more club members than any other sport in Scotland. However, its value is much more profound when you examine the associated health benefits, social and community impact, and the environment. That it can be played 'from cradle to grave', where the handicap system levels the playing field so golfers of all abilities, spanning generations, can play together on an equal basis is an important factor. Golfers walk for miles on each round, in fresh air, contributing to better heart, joint and mental health. Data also suggests golfers live on average five years longer by virtue of playing the sport.

"We also know that the scale of the golf estate can be harnessed to assist in issues around climate change, and that golf clubs are working hard to protect the natural wildlife within their courses and become more environmentally sustainable. We also know that golf clubs can be integral to local communities, where people of all ages, backgrounds and interests can congregate and socialise. Many non-playing members of golf clubs are ex-golfers, keen to maintain connection to their community through the clubhouse space. So, the reach of the sport extends way beyond the fairways, into families, friendships, nature and communities. Truly, it is Scotland's game for everyone."

> It was a great family game for us and still is . . . I love that part of the game. That you can play with anyone and it doesn't matter how good or bad they are at it or what age they are.

CATRIONA MATTHEW

It's when you hear what the game has given to the likes of Matthew, Lawrie and Colin Montgomerie that you realise it's more than just a sport, even though it has provided a good living for all three. "It has given me the best education anyone can ever have, and that education is travel," says Montgomerie, an eight-time European No. 1 and Ryder Cup legend. "The knowledge, the culture, the history and the friendships you make travelling the world. I have also learned a lot more travelling than I ever did in a classroom. Golf has taken me to all six continents on numerous occasions."

Eight-time European No. 1 Colin Montgomerie.

Stephen Gallacher watched by his son/caddie Jack.

Others feel likewise. "Golf has given me a life," declares Andrew Coltart, who played in a Ryder Cup in Boston alongside both Lawrie and Montgomerie before deciding to take his career in golf in a different direction by becoming a highly respected member of the Sky Sports Golf commentary team. "I've got a wonderful wife and three beautiful kids, something to be grateful for and look forward to every day I open my eyes."

"Playing golf is all I ever wanted to do, so I'm the fortunate one," declares Stephen Gallacher, who played in a winning Ryder Cup team at Gleneagles in 2014. "All my best mates are from when we grew up playing golf at Bathgate and I now travel the world with my son, Jack, who is my caddie, which golf has allowed to happen."

It's not just tour stars who feel appreciative of what the game has given them. "It has brought joy to my heart," says David Scott, one of the best-known PGA professionals in Scotland. He now runs Dumbarnie Links after also being involved in getting Kingsbarns Golf Links up and running. "I was a 'poorer than average' pupil at Madras College in St Andrews and left with only five O Levels. I went

Andrew Coltart played in the 1999 Ryder Cup in Boston.

to college to study quantity surveying. In year two, I was bored stiff with the subject and looked for something that I'd at least enjoy. I applied for the assistant pro job at Blairgowrie Golf Club and, within a couple of weeks, I knew that I had found my true vocation. I loved every element of the profession and still do."

Dumbarnie Links general manager David Scott.

SWEET HOME SOIL

In a playing sense, there's nothing that beats tasting victory on Scottish soil. Tom Watson became extremely popular with Scottish golf fans through never hiding what winning in the Home of Golf – he achieved that feat four times in The Open and three times in The Senior Open – meant to him. It was also a proud moment for Rory McIlroy as the Northern Irishman achieved that for the first time when he pipped home hope Robert MacIntyre in the 2023 Genesis Scottish Open at The Renaissance Club.

One of Matthew's Ladies European Tour title triumphs came on home soil in the 1998 McDonald's WPGA Championship at Gleneagles, yet that isn't her best playing memory in Scotland. "It would be from the Women's British Open at St Andrews in 2013, the year Stacy Lewis won, when we had all the wind. I remember going out on the Sunday morning to complete my round and finished 3-2 on 17 and 18 at St Andrews," she recalls with a smile. "That was from a playing point of view, but the 2019 Solheim Cup at Gleneagles, you can't really top that. Being the captain. Having that chance in your home country, which doesn't happen often for a European. And, of course, just the way it finished [Europe beating the United States in a dramatic finish as it came down to the last putt. It was holed by Norwegian Suzann Pettersen after she was handed a surprise captain's pick following a spell where she had barely played]. It looked all afternoon like we weren't going to do it. Then, suddenly, the last three games turned around. Then the scenes afterwards with lots of people celebrating on the green."

Dumbarnie Links.

As well as being Ryder Cup players, Lawrie, Gallacher and Montgomerie have another thing in common. All three won the Alfred Dunhill Links Championship, which is played at Carnoustie, Kingsbarns Golf Links and St Andrews, where the final round is held. Winning there is probably the most special feeling in golf and even more so when it's in either The Open or the AIG Women's Open. Montgomerie finished second to Tiger Woods over the Old Course in 2005 yet it still delivered his favourite memory on a Scottish golf course. "Holing a 30-foot putt on the 18th green on the Saturday to beat Tiger by a shot," he declares of signing for a 70 as the American, who was almost unbeatable at the time, had to settle for a 71.

It's no surprise, of course, that Woods inspired young Scottish golfers but, at the same time, the likes of Matthew, Lawrie and Sandy Lyle in particular as major winners have played their part in making sure that new generations keep coming through in the sport's cradle. "Catriona has been an idol of mine since I was young," admits Gemma Dryburgh, the new leading light in the Scottish women's game. "She has been kind enough to give me advice through the years when I was coming up the ranks. To take over as Scottish No. 1 was an amazing feeling and also a huge privilege. I hope I can inspire as many young golfers as she has to take up the game and also push through to the next level."

On the back of his Open win, Lawrie launched a junior foundation in the north-east of Scotland and the template for that was subsequently used by Gallacher as he produced something similar in and around Edinburgh. Flag events introduce youngsters to the game and players are given great opportunities to see how far they can progress. Some become foundation ambassadors and it's certainly not just a case of Lawrie or Gallacher putting names to those projects. They attend events whenever possible and hand over the trophies. Scotland can count itself lucky to have people like them as faces of golf in the country but, at the same time, they admit to feeling lucky about what golf has given them.

Golfers walk for miles on each round, in fresh air, contributing to better heart, joint and mental health.

LGPA Tour winner Gemma Dryburgh.

"I honestly never thought we would achieve any of it," admits Lawrie on getting his hands on the Claret Jug, winning seven other times as a DP World Tour player, making two Ryder Cup appearances and also counting a Scottish PGA Championship among numerous other victories earlier in his career. "When I turned pro, I was 17 playing off a five handicap. I didn't play much golf and I wasn't that good, but that was the limit to being a pro. I didn't think I would be anything other than – and it would have been okay, in fact I'd have been hunky dory with that – a club pro doing repairs and teaching the members. But to get what I have in the end, travelling the world in the process and playing 621 DP World Tour events, is still unbelievable.

"I think when you are not expecting that to happen and you are not very good, you appreciate it a little bit more. When you are really good and hugely talented and people are expecting you to do all those things, it would probably mean a lot, but it certainly means more when you didn't think you would ever do that. It didn't make me any less grumpy when I played poorly, of course! The biggest kick I still get and I find this quite strange is that not every day but, at least once or twice a month, there's still people who come up and ask to shake the hand of an Open champion. I get that all the time. I think it's a wee bit odd, but, at the same time, it's really cool."

> The reach of the sport extends way beyond the fairways, into families, friendships, nature and communities. Truly, it is Scotland's game for everyone.

ROBBIE CLYDE

The Paul Lawrie and Stephen Gallacher Foundations have helped grow golf in Scotland.

3

SCOTLAND IS WHERE GOLF STARTED

St Andrews-based golf historian Roger McStravick.

Imagine being a golf historian. Imagine being a golf historian based in Scotland. Imagine being a golf historian living in St Andrews. Step forward Roger McStravick, an award-winning author, who still wakes up every morning feeling a tinge of excitement about penning fascinating tales about some of the key figures in the game in its birthplace.

"It has been an absolute joy," says McStravick, who specialises in St Andrews, Old Tom Morris and other legends from the 1880s through to 1920. "St Andrews has wonderful archives. The R&A and the University of St Andrews have the most amazing collections, as do the St Andrews Preservation Trust, in terms of images of 19th-century St Andrews. I have particularly enjoyed researching people. Be it Allan Robertson, Tom Morris or Sir Hugh Lyon Playfair, their lives were quite remarkable and the changes they made, whether it was on the links or in St Andrews, resonate with us still today."

Old and Young Tom Morris

John Rattray's statue on Leith Links.

Myth has it that Mary Stuart, better known as Mary Queen of Scots, played golf at Musselburgh in 1567, but there is definitive evidence that Sir John Foulis, a prominent Edinburgh lawyer, had a game there in 1672. The course at Musselburgh was originally just seven holes and it was a local blacksmith, Robert Gay, who made a device for cutting holes, which eventually became the standard size in 1893.

Golf officially became a sport on Leith Links in 1744. A bronze statue of Dr John Rattray, the first captain of the Leith Rules of Golf Society, has been in place on the north side of the Links since 2019, while a plaque nearby shows the first set of rules that were drawn up for the game, which quickly spread through the rest of Scotland.

David Hamilton, regarded as the "Godfather of Golf History" on the strength of his unrivalled knowledge of the subject, wrote *Golf, Scotland's Game*, which, according to those who know, is still likely to be read in a hundred years' time. "As a surgeon in Glasgow, I had been writing a lot on medical history and I was impressed with how badly golf history

"Godfather of Golf History", David Hamilton.

had been neglected," he says. "It was stuck in the shepherds hitting pebbles with their crooks nonsense and that Mary Queen of Scots used her handicap of two when visiting St Andrews. Using my other history experience, I knew where to look for better sources and better insights. The book was a success because I uncovered so much about 'golf' before the famous clubs were founded in the 1700s and there was also plenty of humble golf outside these gentlemen's societies. A surprise was that it was a winter game, since the summer was too

important in an agricultural nation."

Over time, he's even managed to persuade the Dutch that the game was invented in Scotland and not, as often claimed over the years, in the Netherlands. "Yes, I'm beginning to win the argument that golf evolved from the shinty which we played from Columba's time onwards," he adds. "We played first at what I call 'short golf' with the home-made shinty equipment. Then Scotland's well-off great and good, always seeking distance to beat the king, developed modern golf (which I call 'long golf' to separate it from 'short golf'), ordered expensive artisan-made clubs and expensive feather balls. We in Scotland too readily assumed that Scottish golf must have come from Europe – the usual Scottish cringe – and this was underpinned because Europe had better images and literary descriptions of their stick-and-ball game. However, the European historians are rolling over because they understandably didn't know about shinty."

Allan Robertson and Tom Morris, by T. Hodge c1889.
From an illustration about golf, dating from 1889 to 1901.

GOLF'S ICONS OF AULD

Lots of towns and villages are now steeped in history when it comes to golf, but it's St Andrews, where the first reference to it was in 1552, that is widely regarded as its cradle. Hence why the likes of Hamilton and McStravick (who worked for VisitScotland, the national tourism bureau, before getting his teeth into writing and displaying a true passion for golf), have based much of their work on either the Auld Grey Toun itself or those who were influenced by spending time there and being involved in the sport in its formative years. The likes of the aforementioned Robertson, for example, who blazed the trail as a professional golfer, both in a playing sense and also as a golf ball maker. Old Tom Morris, arguably the most famous name in the game's history, started out doing an apprenticeship under Robertson.

"I am writing a biography of Allan Robertson and what that has showed me is that every generation over the 600 years that golf has been played, encourages the next," says McStravick, a double winner of the Herbert Warren Wind Award named after a legendary American golf writer and presented annually by the United States Golf Association, one of the sport's governing bodies, as well as being a recipient of the British Golf Collectors' Society Murdoch Medal.

"The list of Scottish names of those who were pivotal is very long. Allan's father was the Champion golfer, but it is Allan's death that led to the creation of The Open. A Scot called Dr Montgomerie was credited for bringing gutta percha to the country, and that revolution-ised the golf ball industry leading to a massive growth in the game. Tom Morris created over a hundred courses and his green-keeping techniques are still in use today. In terms of the development of the game, Tom is probably the most pivotal. He was a supporter of ladies' golf and embraced new technology. As the game was opening up across Scotland and into England, Tom's knowledge was called upon. It was also the excitement he created on the links with his matches against Willie Park. His body of work led to an expansion of the ability to play golf, sound maintenance of links and also public interest in the game. He is Scotland's most iconic golf figure for good reason."

Myth has it that Mary Stuart, better known as Mary Queen of Scots, played golf at Musselburgh in 1567.

Sean Connery, of course, loved his golf and his son, Jason, directed *Tommy's Honour*, a film depicting the lives and careers of both Old and Young Tom that won Best Feature Film at the 2016 British Academy Scotland Awards. Peter Mullan, a well-known Scottish actor, played Old Tom while compatriot Jack Lowden was Young Tom. The cast also included Sam Neill as Alexander Boothby, captain of the Royal & Ancient Golf Club of St Andrews. Both in terms of researching and writing, McStravick takes great pride in *St Andrews in the Footsteps of Old Tom Morris*, which was the first of his books to win the aforementioned Herbert Warren Wind Award.

"My son was two at the time, so I wrote it when he slept," he recalls. "I wanted a visual book like Andy Hall's beautiful *A Sense of Belonging to Scotland* combined with new historical research. History books traditionally have wonderful images but are tiny postage stamps in size. Chic Harper, the designer, more than achieved what I was hoping for and created a beautiful book with *Footsteps*. On the research side, I am happiest back in the 19th century. With *Footsteps* I was trying to capture everything that they could see. For example, what was the links like before they reclaimed the West Sands beach and created land, which

would become the first hole and what did they feel like at the time, be it Playfair's changes to the town, cholera outbreaks or early demises. Spending three years researching *Footsteps* was a joyful burden."

Old Tom's grave in the churchyard of St Andrews Cathedral – his son, Young Tom, is also buried there – has been visited by hundreds of thousands of golf aficionados over the years and, fittingly, a new tribute to Old Tom in the shape of a monument on The Scores embankment at the back of the R&A Clubhouse is being planned by the Old Tom Statue Project Group.

"The genesis of the idea came about by accident," says Ronald Sandford, the group's chair. "There was a move afoot a few years ago to hold an annual 'Old Tom Morris Golf Day'. Two friends and I volunteered to represent the Crail Golfing Society and did so at places like Tain, Lossiemouth and, maybe 10 years ago, Rosapenna in Donegal. It was at Rosapenna that we came across a magnificent statue of Old Tom." Referring, in contrast, to how he'd been remembered in St Andrews, Sandford adds: "There is an inherent modesty in Old Tom. Look at his grave. It is marked by what is little more than a flat stone. In contrast, Young Tom's right next door is like a shrine. So this

Screengrab from *Tommy's Honour*, directed by Jason Connery.

> In terms of the development of the game,
> Tom Morris is probably the most pivotal.

ROGER McSTRAVICK

Big St Andrews fan Christy O'Connor jnr.

recognition is timely."

One of my everlasting memories in golf is speaking to Irishman Christy O'Connor Jnr during the 2000 Open at St Andrews and listening to him say it was the only venue in the world where he declined a courtesy car because a walk to wherever he was staying in the town allowed him to soak up its special atmosphere, as numerous others are happy to testify.

"St Andrews is a time machine," says McStravick. "You literally can walk in the footsteps of legends. Around the town, the homes of the 19th-century legends like Tom Morris and his son Tommy, are all still there. You can stand in the same spot where Tom stood on the links, as future prime minister of the UK AJ Balfour played as captain of the R&A. Having that ability makes it easier to imagine. Where Tommy's wife died during childbirth, their house is still there at Albany Place. Where Jamie Anderson lived when he won three Opens in a row is still there at 9 The Links. You can even stay there! It is a truly special place and I am always finding something new."

And not just out on the streets. Even in recent years, golf historians can still stumble over something during their research that sends a tingle of excitement through their body. Recalling one such moment, McStravick says: "When at the University of St Andrews Special Collections department, I came across a pile of folded documents. As I gently opened them up, I realised that they were statements by the people of 19th-century St Andrews. More than that, the names were incredible, like Tom Morris, Bob Martin and Jamie Anderson. They were all talking about their earliest memories of St Andrews and what they thought about the idea of putting a road down the

> "The barriers to women becoming members came crashing down like the Berlin Wall. And guess what? The world still continues to turn."
>
> SHONA MALCOLM

side of the links, which is The Links road today. That was by far the most exciting discovery as no one had ever written about these statements and rather than someone describing Old Tom's life, here he was talking about it himself. He clearly set out and answered a few things that until that point had only been guessed at. From those papers, I wrote *St Andrews: The Road War Papers*, which also won the USGA book award. It was and still is exciting to look at those. The university archives are truly special."

Musselburgh was once certified as being the oldest golf course in the world by Guinness World Records before that honour was reassigned to St Andrews on the basis of the first reference to golf on the Old Course being in 1552, as previously mentioned. On most lists, the 1562 Course at Montrose Links is the second oldest, followed by the Golf House Club Elie (1589), Musselburgh Old (1672), Fortrose & Rosemarkie (1702), Kingsbarns Golf Links (1793), Kinghorn (1812), Scotscraig (1817), North Berwick West Links (1832) and Carnoustie Golf Links (1839). In essence, it was a game that started in the east of the country, although there is an early reference to golf on Glasgow Green in 1721, with Prestwick and Lanark both being added to the list in 1851 as golf's popularity started to spread.

The golf course at Musselburgh sits inside the racecourse in the East Lothian town.

SOCIETIES OF GOLFERS

Courses are one thing but societies, as they were referred to at the outset, and clubs are another when it comes to historic lists. In that respect, Royal Burgess in Edinburgh, which was established in 1735, is the world's oldest society, closely followed by the Honourable Company of Edinburgh Golfers (1744), the Royal & Ancient Golf Club of St Andrews (1754) and Bruntsfield Links Golfing Society (1761). Royal Burgess and Bruntsfield Links are now neighbours on the outskirts of the capital but Bruntsfield Links, where the society started and golf is documented in 1695, is located in the heart of the city, with golf still being played there over a 36-hole short course. Royal Blackheath was the first club to be established outside Scotland; it dates back to 1766 before a flood started north of the border as Royal Musselburgh (1774), Fraserburgh (1777), Royal Aberdeen (1780), Crail Golfing Society (1786), Glasgow Golf Club (1787), Earlsferry Golf Society (1787) and Burntisland Golf Club (1791) all came into existence in a relatively short period of time.

There's a real sense of feeling you are getting a taste of golf from yesteryear at all those venues and lots of others, too, though not necessarily by playing on the original courses. Not many, in fact, have remained in the same place. Only the Royal & Ancient Golf Club of St Andrews and the Musselburgh clubs were able to develop and play continuously over their original golfing grounds. Why? Because the majority of the other courses were ploughed up by tenant farmers, meaning other sites had to be sought, though in the case of two courses, Scotscraig and Kingsbarns Links, play resumed on the original sites. That happened fairly quickly in the case of Scotscraig but not at Kingsbarns Links. Willie Auchterlonie laid out the original course there only for it to be mined during the Second World War as part of a national security defence campaign. It then reopened in 2000 after American architect Kyle Phillips created a spectacular modern links, which, in addition to becoming one of three venues used for the Alfred Dunhill Links Championship on an annual basis in the men's professional game, hosted the AIG Women's Open in 2017.

Bruntsfield Short Hole Golf Club on The Meadows in Edinburgh.

There's a real sense of feeling you are getting a taste of golf from yesteryear.

As you might expect, numerous historic moments were recorded over the years. After all, previous play had been referenced as match play – golfers playing on a head-to-head basis and the match being determined on holes won or lost. Stroke play was introduced for the first time in 1759, creating the system where the score on each individual hole in a round is added up. Having a card and pencil in your hand as you head out in a competition is one of the greatest tests in sport and is often mentioned as playing a part in shaping the character of individuals away from a golf course.

The earliest recorded reference to a women's competition was at Musselburgh in 1810 while The Ladies Golf Club of St Andrews was founded in 1867 before becoming the St Andrews Ladies Putting Club. Its members play on The Himalayas along with members of the public, many of whom are non-golfers but love getting the chance to feel as though they've had a taste of the sport in the town while also perhaps paying a visit to the R&A World Golf Museum, a splendid attraction close to the Old Course.

The Clubhouse of St Andrews Ladies Putting Club, overlooking the Himalayas.

In recent times, the all-male barriers at some of Scotland's best-known clubs have been dispensed with. The Royal & Ancient Golf Club of St Andrews led the way by announcing the move to a mixed membership in 2000, with the likes of Royal Troon, Royal Aberdeen, Royal Burgess, Bruntsfield Links, Glasgow, Panmure and Muirfield all following suit – though, in the case of the latter, it took two attempts for the members of the Honourable Company of Edinburgh Golfers to be persuaded to take the step.

"Some of them had to be dragged kicking and screaming into the modern world, with more than one having to go back to their membership on a number of occasions before the barriers to women becoming members came crashing down like the Berlin Wall. And guess what? The world still continues to turn," says Shona Malcolm, CEO of the Ladies Golf Union at the time of those hugely significant changes. "Fast forward to today and it's fair to say that those historic, traditionally male golf clubs have leapfrogged most of the mixed gender clubs in their attitudes to members of the female variety. They don't differentiate their membership by gender – members are members, with no reference at all to whether they are men or women. This is a refreshing move, which many mixed gender clubs could learn from, as they still differentiate, as they always have, by continuing to pay lip service to gender equality and treating men and women differently on a daily basis."

> "St Andrews is a time machine. You literally can walk in the footsteps of legends."
>
> ROGER McSTRAVICK

The Old Course at St Andrews with the R&A Clubhouse and Hamilton Grand in the distance.

4

A COURSE
COLLECTION
SECOND TO
NONE

Some lucky people have played all, or almost all, of the golf courses in Scotland. For the vast majority, though, just sampling the delights on offer when it comes to the collection of golf courses in Scotland is both satisfying and fulfilling. Which should come as no surprise when you start delving into exactly what is on offer in the country, not only in terms of world-renowned links layouts but also inland beauties and hidden gems.

It's those seaside links, of course, that so many golfing visitors to Scotland want to get out on. For many, it's something that is completely alien to them as they tackle rugged linksland running through sand dunes. "It's the uncertainty of how a ball will react when landing on hard, tight ground," says David Scott, the general manager at Dumbarnie Links, one of the country's newest courses, in Fife. "It's the incredible distance someone can hit the ball when landing those firm surfaces. It's the lack of distance when playing into a 40mph zephyr. It's the use of the putter from 40 paces or so from the green, which is unheard of in most countries around the world."

Prestwick Golf Club.

In the main, the pecking order in terms of the most popular courses in the country when it comes to those visitors has been determined by The Open, golf's oldest major and forever synonymous with Scotland. Prestwick, where the event was first held in 1860, has long since fallen off the list of courses used by the R&A for The Open, but the Ayrshire venue remains relevant to those keen to follow in the footsteps of Old Tom Morris, Young Tom Morris, Willie Park Snr and others. In 2022, the original 12-hole course was recreated by the club to mark the 150th Open being held that year across the other side of the country in St Andrews. "It seemed like a good idea at the time," quips Ken Goodwin, the Prestwick secretary at the time, of five of the greens on the recreated course being on what are now fairways and the other one having been relaid in the rough, before adding that it had been achieved thanks to the greenkeeping team "approaching the task with gusto".

Having been another venue where The Open was held in its formative stages, coupled with it being the oldest course in the world, Musselburgh – or Musselburgh Old, as it's better known by the majority of Scots – is also popular with golfing aficionados, but it's those courses that now host The Open that get the most traffic. Top of that list is the Old Course at St Andrews, where the Championship was

first played in 1873 and attracted a record crowd of 290,000 for that milestone 150th edition in 2022, when Australian Cameron Smith got his hands on the coveted Claret Jug.

The Old Course shares a chunk of land that stretches out from the west end of the town towards the Eden Estuary with five other courses, with some people reckoning that its nearest neighbour, the New, is actually a better all-round test of golf. Several top professionals, including Englishman Lee Westwood, have freely admitted to disliking or even hating the Old Course when playing it for the first time but, in most cases, it gradually grows on people. Teeing off in front of one of the game's most iconic buildings, the Royal & Ancient Clubhouse, is one of the special treats in golf, as is walking up the 18th hole as you arrive back in the town and get goosebumps when you think of the game's greats all having made that journey. In between, it will have been almost impossible to

stay out of some of the smallest yet most treacherous bunkers you are likely to ever come across and, of course, also have tackled the Road Hole, one of the game's best-known holes and a potential card-wrecker. Just ask Japanese professional Tsuneyuki 'Tommy' Nakajima, who was in contention in The Open in 1978 until he putted into the bunker at the 17th in the third round, needed four shots to escape from it and signed for a 9 on his scorecard. It was duly dubbed the 'Sands of Nakajima'.

It's neither cheap nor easy to play what, for many, is golf's Holy Grail. In 2024, it cost £320 for an adult in the height of the season and, due to such high demand, there's a ballot system. Until a new digital system was recently introduced, those who missed out on that had an option of trying to secure a walk-up tee time, which could become available through a variety of reasons, and it was common practice for golfers to come out of the pubs in the town at

Tournament officials and greenkeepers at St Andrews.

Carnoustie Golf Links.

closing time and head straight to the golf course to queue overnight. Yes, that's exactly what it means to people to seek out an opportunity that lots of others around the world can perhaps only dream about.

"I defy anyone not to have the hairs stand up on the back of their neck as they tee it up on the first at the Old Course or stand on the Swilcan Bridge on the 18th, where every legend of the game at one point before has crossed," says Alan Tait, one of Scotland's

best-known PGA professionals and also familiar to a wider golfing audience through his after-dinner speaking in the UK.

Similar treats are on offer at those other current venues for The Open and the AIG Women's Open. Since being restored to the R&A list after a spell in the wilderness, the Championship Course at Carnoustie has gone from strength to strength in recent years, which is testament to its management committee. The Angus venue has been the scene

Muirfield, East Lothian.

of a memorable day for the Scottish game as Paul Lawrie, who started out as a PGA assistant selling Mars bars in the pro shop at Banchory, became Open champion in 1999 after trailing by ten shots heading into the final round. The Aberdonian's 4-iron from 221 yards to four feet at the 18th hole in a four-hole play-off was one of the finest blows ever struck on a Scottish course. This meant so much to the local boy: Lawrie lived just an hour or so away from the scene of his finest hour and became the first Scot to triumph in the event on home soil for 68 years.

Muirfield, home of the Honourable Company of Edinburgh Golfers, is regarded by many to be the best of any of The Open courses. The test on the East

Teeing off in front of one of the game's most iconic buildings, the Royal & Ancient Clubhouse, is one of the special treats in golf.

Lothian course comprises an opening nine where the holes circle clockwise around the perimeter of the property then the back nine runs anti-clockwise on an inner circuit. It means the direction of the holes is constantly changing, with a roll of honour that includes the names of Harry Vardon, James Braid (twice), Walter Hagen, Henry Cotton, Gary Player, Jack Nicklaus, Lee Trevino, Tom Watson, Nick Faldo (twice), Ernie Els and Phil Mickelson – all indicating that the cream always comes to the top here.

That was certainly the case when Watson, the eventual winner, and Nicklaus fought out their infamous "Duel in the Sun" at Turnberry in 1977. And it was also a memorable edition just up the Ayrshire coast at Royal Troon in 2016, when Henrik Stenson came out on top in a titanic tussle with Phil Mickelson, the Swede creating history in the process as the first Scandinavian to claim a men's major.

Flanked by the Firth of Clyde on one side and the Glasgow to Ayr railway line on the other, Royal Troon is a terrific test of golf, with the Postage Stamp, a short but tricky par-3 hole, being one of the best in the country. It has long been host to the final round of the Helen Holm Trophy, a top women's amateur event, and, though with no crowds in attendance due to Covid restrictions at the time, it also staged the AIG Women's Open for the first time in 2020, when German Sophia Popov, who was outside the world's top 300 at the time and winless at the top level in her professional career until that point, pulled off a stunning success.

> "It's the uncertainty of how a ball will react when landing on hard, tight ground.
>
> DAVID SCOTT

Muirfield, East Lothian.

Tom Watson came close to doing likewise back at Turnberry in 2009, when, at the age of 59, the man who had won the hearts of so many Scottish fans over the years was on the brink of becoming the game's oldest major winner only to stumble at the 72nd hole before losing in a play-off to his fellow American, Stewart Cink. It wasn't fair on Cink, but it's fair to say that he didn't have many people cheering him on over those closing holes. Grown men were close to tears as Watson came up agonisingly short in his bid to pull off one of the greatest sporting feats in history – a feat which was put into context when Phil Mickelson created a new record in that respect at the age of 50 when winning the PGA Championship in the United States in 2021.

Since that 2009 event, the Ailsa Course at Turnberry has undergone a major renovation, which has turned a good course into a great one. At the same time, though, it found itself in the wilderness in the eyes of the R&A after being bought by Donald Trump. The concern was that golf-mad Trump, who also owns a top-class championship course outside Aberdeen that opened in 2012, would overshadow tournaments there – a gamble the St Andrews-based organisation just wasn't prepared to take in protecting not only championships but also the course itself and the players.

Ailsa Course, Trump Turnberry.

BEYOND THE OPEN

Just below those courses used for The Open are a level of venues that some might even say are just as good. Royal Dornoch in Sutherland, for example, is one of Watson's favourite places to swing a club and enjoy the surroundings. "It's the most fun I've ever had on a golf course," he once said while, in an equally complimentary tone, renowned golf writer Herbert Warren Wind declared that "no golfer has completed his education until he has played and studied Royal Dornoch".

Nairn, venue for wins for Great Britain & Ireland in both the Walker Cup and Curtis Cup – amateur team events against the United States – in 1999 and 2012 respectively, is another outstanding links test; as are Royal Aberdeen, where Englishman Justin Rose won the Scottish Open in 2014, the 1562 Course at Montrose, Monifieth Links, Panmure, Lundin, Leven Links, Gullane, North Berwick, Dunbar and Kilspindie on the east coast and the likes of Kilmarnock (Barassie), Western Gailes, Dundonald Links, Gailes Links and West Kilbride on the west side of the country.

Royal Dornoch.

And let's not forget about some of the new additions to the list of courses: Kingsbarns Golf Links in Fife is now near the top of every bucket list for American visitors in particular, and that's despite the regular green fee there believed to be the most expensive in the country at £418. Originally opened as Castle Stuart but now called Cabot Highlands, the Inverness venue also has a great name in terms of an overall golfing experience. Likewise the aforementioned Dumbarnie Links, where the course was designed by Clive Clark, a former professional who co-commentated with Peter Alliss for the BBC, has quickly established itself as a very popular place to play while enjoying stunning views across the Firth of Forth towards East Lothian and Edinburgh.

Castle Stuart has hosted the Scottish Open in the past, which has now found a new home at The Renaissance Club in East Lothian, where the course – its signature hole includes Fidra, a tiny uninhabited island with a lighthouse on it as a stunning backdrop – was designed by American Tom Doak. It sits next door to Archerfield Links, where the Fidra Links is a fabulous mix of open and tree-lined holes and the neighbouring Dirleton Links is another splendid test of golf. The practice facilities at both The Renaissance Club and Archerfield Links are among the best on offer in Scotland.

As for those inland courses, the most popular destination for many when they venture away from the coast is Gleneagles, home of one of Scotland's premier hotels and three – four if you add in an academy one – fabulous courses that are set in the midst of beautiful scenery in picturesque Perthshire at the north end of Glen Devon. Both the King's and Queen's Courses have long been favourites, with the former having hosted numerous top events, including the Scottish Open at the time when it was sponsored by whisky company Bell's.

The third course was designed by Jack Nicklaus, the game's greatest player, and opened as the Monarch's before being rebranded as the PGA Centenary Course. It hosted the Ryder Cup in 2014 and the Solheim Cup five years later, with both events proving a huge success and resulting in wins for European teams led by Paul McGinley and Catriona Matthew respectively.

Loch Lomond, where former Open champion Tom Weiskopf was involved in its design, is another of the country's top inland layouts. It is ultra-exclusive, with the vast majority of Scots having to settle for visits as golf fans. It hosted a DP World Tour event under a number of guises over a 15-year period and the Solheim Cup in 2000, when a Scot, Dale Reid, led Europe to victory. That biennial event was held for the first time on British soil eight years earlier at Dalmahoy, where the James Braid-designed East Course on the outskirts of Edinburgh is another example of Scotland not necessarily being just about links golf when it comes to good places to play.

> I defy anyone not to have the hairs stand up on the back of their neck as they tee it up on the first at the Old Course or stand on the Swilcan Bridge on the 18th.

ALAN TAIT

King's Course, Gleneagles.

The same goes for Blairgowrie, with its two tree-lined heathland beauties – the Lansdowne and Rosemount – and also the wonderful 'Wee Course'; Ladybank in the heart of Fife; the Dave Thomas-designed Spey Valley in Aviemore; and Boat of Garten, which is arguably one of the most enjoyable places in the whole country to be hitting golf shots. The combination of Garten's location alongside the River Spey with the Cairngorms nearby and the sumptuous test that was shaped by the extraordinary James Braid makes it a unique course.

Snowy scene at Gleneagles.

IN PRAISE OF HIDDEN GEMS

What actually constitutes a "hidden gem" is always a matter of opinion and open for debate. My hidden gems have to include Eyemouth. It's where it all started for me in golf and what is now the sixth hole on the course that sits on the Berwickshire coast is one of the most spectacular in the country due to the tee being on the one side of a huge gully and the green being perched on the other. For some, it's just a case of hit and hope – and for everyone, finding that putting surface is hugely rewarding.

Staying on the east side of the country, Aberdour, my home club since moving to Fife, is another lesser-known but popular venue – and no wonder when you factor in stunning views from almost every hole over towards Edinburgh and Inchcolm. The latter is widely regarded as the most beautiful of the islands in the Firth of Forth and tourists can take a trip there on the *Maid of the Forth* from its base in South Queensferry.

A nine-holer at Anstruther and Crail, with its two courses, including the historic Balcomie Links, are other hidden gems in the Kingdom of Fife, as are the likes of Murcar Links, Cruden Bay, Moray Old and Cullen Links in the north-east, and also Brora and Golspie on the journey north from Inverness to John o' Groats, the most northerly mainland point in the

The 6th hole at Eyemouth Golf Club from the tee (above) and the air (right).

British Isles. Southerness is the pick of courses in the southwest of the country, where Stranraer and Portpatrick are also worth a visit, as is Lanark, the world's oldest inland course and a classic moorland test, in the heart of the Central Belt. And not forgetting Machrihanish Dunes and Dunaverty, home of both legendary Scottish amateur Belle Robertson and Jock MacVicar, the doyen of Scottish golf writers, on the Kintyre peninsula.

Which brings us on nicely to some of the island courses on the west coast, starting on Islay, where The Machrie, having undergone a redesign by DJ

Russell, a former tour player, is the centre-piece of a top-class resort. Shiskine, a 12-holer – yes, that is unusual – set in a stunning location at Blackwaterfoot, is one of seven courses on Arran, while a highly rated Ardfin sits on the southern tip of Jura. Add in Askernish on South Uist, and Traigh, the most westerly course on the mainland between Arisaig and Mallaig, and it's no wonder that the popularity of playing remote courses has been on the up in recent years. Stromness on Orkney and Asta on Shetland merit mention as well as does Durness, which nestles on the north coast.

Remember me saying that some people have been lucky enough to have played most of Scotland's courses? Well, Edinburgh man Allan Shaw clocked up course No. 551 on his personal list by playing Lilliesleaf in the Borders early in 2024, leaving him just 30 to go. "What a great summary to this chapter, giving a flavour of the wide variety of courses in the haven of golf which is Scotland," observes Shaw. "Do not be offended if you are one of the 520 or so that have not been named. That would have taken up the whole book. Be assured that you have all left an indelible memory on everyone that has had the good fortune of having played your course. I always nominate a favourite hole and that is an initial talking point whenever I meet one of your members. There are also many other memories like being chased off the Stornoway course on a summer's evening by the midges! Will have to go back sometime to play the last three . . .

Ardfin Golf Course on the Ardfin Estate, Isle of Jura,

5

CELEBRATING
SCOTTISH
SUCCESS

Sandy Lyle celebrates winning
The Masters in 1988.

Scots celebrate, cherish and categorise success on a golf course like no other country. It's because we care about golf. It's because we gave the game to the world. It's because we are a wee nation and love punching above our weight every now and again.

Look at the record books and you'll see we were spoiled at the start, certainly in terms of The Open as it fell to a Scot in all of its first 29 editions, with pride of place going to Willie Park Snr, Old Tom Morris and Young Tom Morris as they all registered four victories. Jamie Anderson and Bob Ferguson didn't do badly either with three wins apiece, both achieving the feat with a hat-trick of triumphs.

It wasn't until 1890 that the Scottish run of success came to end – English amateur John Ball was the man responsible for that happening – but, after a spell when the great Harry Vardon and JH Taylor shared domination of the event, the Saltire was soon flying high again as James Braid went on to record a remarkable five victories over a ten-year period, culminating at St Andrews as he won by four shots from compatriot Sandy Herd.

Bearing in mind that was back in 1910, it could easily be viewed as disappointing that the event has subsequently produced just four Scottish successes – George Duncan in 1920, Tommy Armour

Paul Lawrie and family show off the Claret Jug in 1999.

in 1931, Sandy Lyle in 1985 and, most recently, Paul Lawrie in 1999 – but, at the same time, it's important to put that into context. First and foremost, the game started to grow elsewhere in the United Kingdom and across the Atlantic in the United States in the first instance, and then to other corners of the globe. Scotland may still be the Home of Golf, but it's no longer the powerhouse it once was in a playing sense.

The 18th hole, Royal Dornoch.

GOLF'S HISTORY MAKERS

That said, several have done their bit
over the years to keep giving us Scots
something to shout about, with Lyle –
Alexander Walter Barr Lyle, to give him
his full name – certainly doing that on a
couple of occasions. He won the Claret
Jug at Royal St George's in 1985, providing one of the most memorable days
in the rich history of the Scottish game,
and his 7-iron shot from a fairway bunker
at the 72nd hole in The Masters in 1988
earned him a place in the event's folklore.
His setting up of a closing birdie saw Lyle
create history as the first British golfer
to have a Green Jacket, the most-prized
piece of clothing in golf, if not sport,
slipped over his shoulders.

"It probably won't come as a surprise
for me to say that I play with guys in
pro-ams most weeks who remember that
bunker shot and that is nice," admits Lyle,
who made his 42nd and final appearance

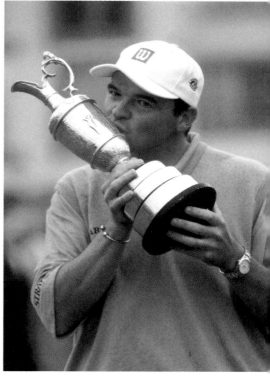

Paul Lawrie wins the 1999 British Open Golf
Championship at Carnoustie.

in the Augusta National event in 2023, having created history the previous year as the first Scottish player to clock up outings in a hundred majors. "It's not everyone who has produced a shot that has made an impact like that on people," he says.

Tiger Woods greeted his return to winning ways on the very same stage in 2019 with an almighty roar, but, for Lyle, it had been a sort of shy shuffle as he celebrated his winning putt down the slope. "It wasn't quite ready to get me on *Strictly Come Dancing*, let's put it that way," he recalls, laughing. "To be honest, I was just basically out on my feet because the last two or three holes were probably like running a marathon. In my head, I was probably thinking that I would do a somersault on the green if I won but my legs had gone and my arms were heavy, so that's the best I could manage. To be honest, I could just have sat down in that spot for a couple of minutes and soaked up the occasion."

Lawrie did exactly that when he joined Lyle in becoming a major winner, and not just because it was wet that afternoon at Carnoustie, as he delivered the first success by a Scottish-born player on home soil in The Open for 68 years. Armour, nick-named the Silver Scot, was still flying the Saltire when he landed his victory at the same venue before becoming an American citizen a few years later. By that time, he'd also landed wins in the US Open and PGA

Alexander Walter Barr Lyle created history as the first British golfer to earn the honour of wearing a Green Jacket.

Dunbar Golf Club.

Cabot Highlands, Inverness.

Championship, making him one of just three UK natives – Jim Barnes and Rory McIlroy are the others – to have claimed three different men's majors.

Too much is still made of Jean van de Velde making a hash of the 72nd hole – he had his socks and shoes off contemplating hitting a shot from the Barry Burn – in Lawrie's Open win. Yes, the Frenchman should probably have triumphed, but the record books don't lie and Lawrie deserves way more credit than he gets. The Aberdonian came from ten shots behind heading into the final round. He closed with a best-of-the-day 67 at a venue frequently dubbed Carnasty due to it being widely regarded as the toughest championship course in the world. He played out of his skin in a four-hole play off against both Van de Velde and American Justin Leonard. The boy done good. No, make that very good!

"The Open at Carnoustie in 1999 will always be my greatest achievement in golf," says Lawrie. To have your name on the Claret Jug is still something you struggle to explain to people. It's still hard to believe your name is actually on there and I'm the last man from Scotland to win a major. I don't want that to be the case. People think I dine out on that, but it's the absolute opposite. I want Bob [Robert] MacIntyre to win a major. I want David Law to win a major. Why would you not? But what happened that day and that week, you will never get tired of talking about it and the fact it was an hour from my house and I drove home that night with the Claret Jug in the back seat of the car is Cinderella stuff."

> 66
> The Open at Carnoustie in 1999 will always
> be my greatest achievement in golf.
> 99
>
> PAUL LAWRIE

A GLITTERING PROFESSIONAL CAREER

2009 AIG Women's Open winner Catriona Matthew.

Another magical major moment was delivered by Catriona Matthew, who is up there with the likes of Andy Murray in tennis and Chris Hoy in cycling in terms of her overall success in the game of golf and, of course, for being a fabulous ambassador for her country in the process. Taken purely at face value, her title triumph in the Women's British Open at Royal Lytham in 2009 was praiseworthy on its own. Factor in, though, that she created history as the first Scot to land a women's major just 11 weeks after giving birth to her second daughter and it is easy to see why the North Berwick woman created the legend of the golfing "Supermum".

Europe celebrates winning the 2019 Solheim Cup at Gleneagles.

She's also now a Solheim Cup legend. After making nine playing appearances in the biennial contest against the United States, Matthew led Europe to victory on home soil at Gleneagles in 2019 before repeating the feat two years later in Tulsa. To put that into context, she's the only European captain to have achieved the feat and did so by having the full respect of her players on both occasions. She may be the quiet type, but don't let that fool you. A winning mentality has helped Matthew secure her place among the greats of the Scottish game.

"In one way, I'd say my career was slightly disappointing in terms of not winning more on the LPGA," admits a modest Matthew. "You know, I had a lot of chances and a lot of top tens but just couldn't quite find that formula to get into the winning circle more often than I did. On the other hand, when I turned professional back in 1994, I'd never have thought I'd win a major, play in nine Solheim Cups and be a Solheim Cup captain. So, in that respect, I'm really pleased about it being a successful career."

Taken purely at face value, Catriona Matthew's title triumph in the Women's British Open at Royal Lytham in 2009 was praiseworthy on its own.

Ask anyone around the world to name one Scottish golfer and there's a good chance they'll come up with Colin Montgomerie.

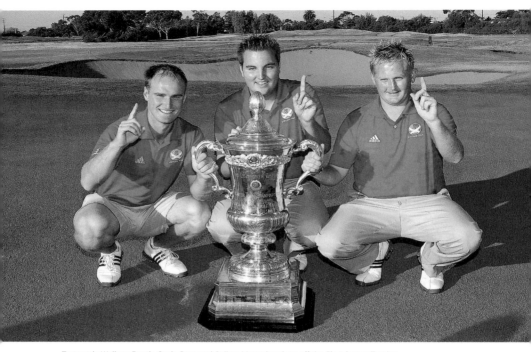

Tartan trio Wallace Booth, Gavin Dear and Callum Macaulay show off the Eisenhower Trophy.

A LEGENDARY TEAM PLAYER

Ask anyone around the world to name one Scottish golfer and there's a good chance they'll come up with Colin Montgomerie. Understandably so. Yes, he'll be disappointed about failing to land a major – no one really counts the senior ones when it comes to analysing careers – and, boy, did it hurt when he let a golden opportunity slip from his grasp at Winged Foot

in 2006, when he missed the green at the 18th hole in the final round with what was a stock shot for him. He also finished second in the sport's showpiece events on four other occasions.

His place as one of the legends of the European game, though, will never be questioned. Not when he was crowned as the European Tour's No. 1 seven years in a row and eight times in total. Not when he racked up 31 titles on the circuit. And not when he was Europe's talisman in the Ryder Cup, leading from the front as he played on five winning teams before captaining the home side to victory at Celtic Manor Resort in South Wales in 2010. Three years after that, he was inducted into the World Golf Hall of Fame, earning that honour in the international ballot at the same time as compatriot Ken Schofield as the former European Tour executive director was voted in through the lifetime achievement category.

"Every time I sit in my study at home and view the eight Harry Vardon Trophies that are on display, [I think] I did okay," says Montgomerie of the prize awarded to the player who tops the Order of Merit on what is now known as the DP World Tour and claimed by Rory McIlroy for a fifth time in 2023. "However, I always enjoyed winning as part of a team, more so than an individual. Helping the team in any way was always a greater thrill, whether it be Ryder Cup, Walker Cup, Eisenhower Trophy, World Cup, Seve Trophy and even now on the Champions Tour with the World Champions Cup."

Montgomerie was on top of the world

Stephen Gallacher sits on the Swilcan Bridge after a St Andrews success in the Dunhill Links

when he teamed up with Marc Warren, one of his younger compatriots, to land Scotland's sole success in the World Cup of Golf at Mission Hills in China in 2007. Another notable tartan team triumph was delivered in the amateur ranks in the Eisenhower Trophy in Australia the following year. In an event that had previously seen Scots represent Great Britain & Ireland, Wallace Booth, Gavin Dear and Callum Macaulay joined forces in Adelaide to win by nine shots from a star-studded US side and duly be crowned as world champions.

"It was a while ago now but still a great memory," says Macaulay. "We were really well prepared and we had a great mentality as a team, helped by the positivity of [team manager] George Crawford and [national coach] Ian Rae. We were all playing well and felt confident, with the weather playing into our hands due to it being windy and it being fast, links-style conditions. Looking back, as a tiny nation to go out there and dominate against some top teams was a testament to us all as a group. At the time, being the 'Olympics of golf', it was a fantastic achievement and one we as a country can be very proud of. I hope I'm wrong, but it's unlikely it'll happen again."

Lawrie enjoyed another special moment in his career when winning the inaugural Alfred Dunhill Links

> As a kid, you watch the Scottish team line up and sing the national anthem as the flag flies and now watching the lone piper up on the roof at Murrayfield gives me goosebumps.

RICHIE RAMSAY

Dunhill Links delight for Andrew Coltart, Sam Torrance and Colin Montgomerie.

Championship, a star-studded pro-am event held at Carnoustie, Kingsbarns Links and St Andrews, in 2001. Stephen Gallacher emulated that feat just three years later before Montgomerie did likewise in 2005. "I've got so many great memories from playing golf in Scotland," admits Gallacher. "Playing with my late father Jim and being taken to the golf course by my uncle Bernard. But, other than playing in the Ryder Cup at

Gleneagles in 2014, that was probably my most memorable experience, especially as my late grandad Barney was there to see it."

When it was played as the Dunhill Cup, a team event, Montgomerie linked up with Sam Torrance and Andrew Coltart to land a memorable Scottish success at St Andrews in 1995. There's more than just one reason why that will always be Coltart's favourite memory on a Scottish

Robert MacIntyre teamed up with Justin Rose in the 2023 Ryder Cup in Rome.

Winning Ryder Cup captain Sam Torrance.

course. "Ten years earlier, my father and I snuck out to place my departed grand-father's flat cap behind his favourite tee at the eighth hole," he recalls. "In that Dunhill Cup win, I made a hole-in-one there en route to winning my match and lifting the trophy on the steps behind the 18th green with the R&A clubhouse as a backdrop. It truly is a magical, spiritual place and it doesn't get better than that."

In addition to Montgomerie, Bernard Gallacher and Sam Torrance also tasted victory as European Ryder Cup captains. It was third-time lucky for Gallacher as he got his hands on the trophy at Oak Hill in 1995 while Torrance came up with a winning formula in 2002 at The Belfry, where he'd created one of the event's most iconic moments as he raised his arms in celebration after holing the winning putt against the Americans 17 years earlier. "It had nothing to do with me," insists Torrance in a modest tone of his winning captaincy in a match that was put back by 12 months due to the terrorist attacks in the US. "I led them to the water and they drank copiously. They were led by Monty, who was fantastic all week."

A total of 23 Scots have played in the Ryder Cup, the most recent being Robert MacIntyre, who was part of Luke Donald's winning team in Rome in 2023. "I've only seen my dad in tears a few times and it's for serious reasons, but not on this occasion," says the Oban man of what it had meant to not only him but his family.

Seven Scots, meanwhile, have donned European colours in the Solheim Cup and all but one played on winning teams, including Gemma Dryburgh in Malaga in 2023. "It meant the world to me to make the Solheim Cup team," says the Aberdonian. "It had been a dream of mine to make the team one day ever since I remember first watching it as a junior golfer. I loved team sports growing up, so to have a chance to represent Europe on the golf course was such a privilege."

Scottish success in general may be small these days in comparison to, say, England, which has a much bigger player base, but there's still something special in golf when a Saltire is sitting at the top of a leaderboard, as the likes of new talent in Hannah Darling, Connor Graham, Lorna McClymont and Calum Scott have been striving to do in the amateur ranks, both on the US college circuit and closer to home in domestic events.

Richie Ramsay, a four-time winner on the DP World Tour, spoke of the "incredible pride" that simply comes from a golfer being announced on any tee around the world as representing Scotland. "As a kid, you watch the Scottish team line up and sing the national anthem as the flag flies and now watching the lone piper up on the roof at Murrayfield [venue for Scotland rugby internationals] gives me goosebumps," says the Aberdonian. "We may not have a piper when we stand on the first tee, but I think everybody is still incredibly proud to represent Scotland and have that Saltire next to their name. We're a small but great nation and it's nice to fly the flag for Scotland."

6

SCOTTISH GOLF
GOES GLOBAL

"I just had to play a course built in the 1700s – it blows my mind!" The words of an American overheard on the way to Edinburgh. It was a comment that summed up exactly why Scotland is one of the main golf tourism destinations in the world and, as a consequence, it means that the sport is huge in terms of contributing to the country's economy.

It is estimated that golf tourism in Scotland is responsible for £300 million worth of economic impact each year, making it the biggest tourism sector in sport in Scotland. Out of that £300 million, 52 per cent is domestic travel – someone coming from the east coast to Dundonald Links in Ayrshire, for example, or someone coming from the west to go to St Andrews or Castle Stuart and perhaps staying overnight. There's then about 30 per cent comes from England, the vast majority of which comes from the north of England into the south of Scotland. So Manchester and above and the Newcastle area equates to quite a bit. Over and above that, you've then got five per cent short haul from Europe and then 15 per cent comes from America. However, that 15 per cent spends by far and away the most money and equates to £100 million of the £300 million. So, 15 per cent of the people who come are actually spending 30 per cent of the money because they will stay longer

Gleneagles Hotel.

and spend money at some of the fancier hotels and golf courses.

Prime locations for those well-heeled visitors include Gleneagles, where a luxurious five-star hotel first opened its doors in 1924 and the three courses – the King's, the Queen's and the PGA Centenary – are located in a stunning location at the north end of Glen Devon in picturesque Perthshire. "We are proud to have been recognised as the No. 1 Golf Resort in the UK for a number of years, but we never rest on our laurels; we're continuously striving to further elevate the overall experience," says Conor O'Leary, the managing director. "Our location is important. Gleneagles is in the heart of Scotland, barely an hour's drive from Edinburgh and slightly further from Glasgow, so we are very accessible for Scottish and international visitors."

Regarded as the precursor to the Ryder Cup, Gleneagles hosted the first international golf match between British and American professionals in 1921. It was a magical moment when the Ryder Cup was held there in 2014, when a European team led by Paul McGinley defeated the United States under Tom Watson's leadership. Catriona Matthew enjoyed a memorable week there on home soil five years later as she captained Europe to victory in the Solheim Cup in a thrilling encounter that came down to the final putt on the final green as it was holed by Norwegian Suzann Pettersen. Especially so on a glorious day, there are few better places to swing a golf club, but it offers so much more in terms of its attractiveness to visitors from both home and abroad.

"The array of world-class facilities, experiences and dining options also set us apart, offering guests myriad options once the last putt has dropped," adds O'Leary of the venue that was bought by Ennismore, a London-based developer of unique hospitality properties and experiences, from drinks giant Diageo in 2015. "Where else can you finish a round of golf and head straight to a two-Michelin Star restaurant as you can here with Restaurant Andrew Fairlie."

The Old Course Hotel in St Andrews.

Trump Turnberry.

The Old Course Hotel in St Andrews and the Donald Trump-owned Turnberry Hotel are two other extremely popular destinations at the top end of the golf tourism business in Scotland, while Rusacks in St Andrews, the Marine in both North Berwick and Royal Troon and the Station in Dornoch have also all been transformed since coming under the Marine & Lawn Hotels & Resorts umbrella in recent years; the latter being where many people stay when making the pilgrimage north of Inverness to tackle Royal Dornoch – a course where, after playing three rounds despite initially

planning for his visit to take in just one, Tom Watson once proclaimed it had "been the most fun I've ever had on a golf course".

Located in the Highlands county of Sutherland, Royal Dornoch may be a fair distance from Scotland's main golfing hotbeds, but that doesn't put people off making the journey up the A9, the main arterial road in the northern part of the country. "There's many reasons people come here," says Neil Hampton, the club's long-serving general manager. "It's been lauded as one of the best courses, if not the best in the world. Why do

The 8th hole, Royal Dornoch.

people always search for Royal Dornoch? Real golfers around the world do their research to find out where the best courses are and what they are. And even before people could get here they knew this was great and, therefore, they were going to make that pilgrimage somehow."

"As for what makes Royal Dornoch great, I think it's down to what makes links golf the greatest game in the world, which is due to it being how the game should be played and you are never going to repeat the style of links golf we have. As much as Mike Keiser [founder and owner of America's No. 1 golf destination

Gullane Golf Club's Members' Clubhouse.

Bandon Dunes on the south Oregon coast] and these guys are doing well at building courses, they are never quite what we have as it is nature in its rawest. These great architects – your James Braid and Young Tom Morris – had an eye for looking at the shape and lie of the land and saying. "We'll put a tee here, a green there and we'll maybe put a bunker there.' They could see it."

Journeys to courses in Scotland get the juices flowing. I love driving down the A823 through Glen Devon and seeing Gleneagles Hotel at the bottom framed by the town of Crieff in the backdrop, heading down towards St Andrews on the A915 from Upper Largo and coming round the last bend in Aberlady on the A198 and seeing the magnificent sight of Gullane Hill appear in front of you.

In Hampton's eyes, the drive along the A949 after turning off the A9 to get to Royal Dornoch is equally special. "You come across the Dornoch bridge, turn right off the A9, drive through Camore, come down the hill, past the school and into the main street then you go 'ah, Dornoch'. It was our great friend Nick

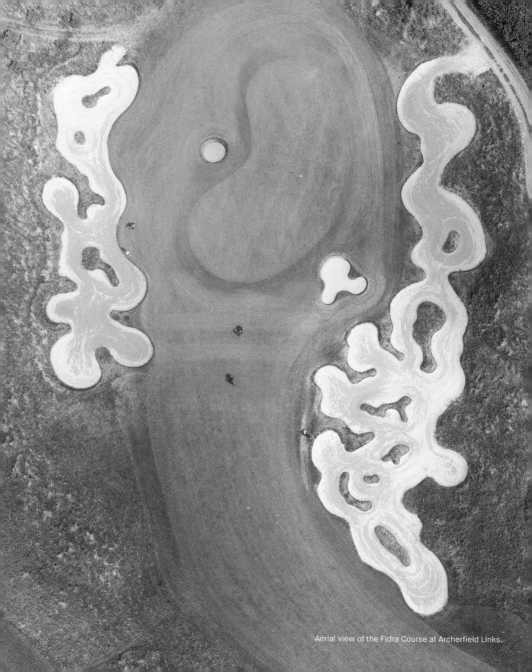

Aerial view of the Fidra Course at Archerfield Links.

The Renaissance Club with Fidra
Island in the background.

Edmund who coined that. He said, "It's not Dornoch; it's ah, Dornoch', and you can feel it as you drive through between the beautiful sandstone buildings and past the cathedral and the castle. Then, as a lot of people mention, as you drive up Golf Road, you can see the flagpoles appearing over the horizon then you see the sign and when you get to the car park, you can see the sea. And, suddenly, it's that wow feeling. Maybe that's part of the mystique as well. The old [renowned golf author] Malcolm Campbell thing that it's not a links course unless you can see the sea, and you can see the sea from every single shot and every single step of the way at Dornoch."

In truth, the title could have been claimed by a number of other areas around the country, but it was a masterstroke when East Lothian became universally known as Scotland's Golf Coast. It claims to have the 'greatest concentration of championship links golf courses in the world', the jewel in the crown being Muirfield, where The Open has been staged on 16 occasions, while the likes of North Berwick, Dunbar, Gullane and Longniddry have long been popular venues for visitors from all over the world. It is also now home to The Renaissance Club, venue for the Genesis Scottish Open since 2019, and neighbouring Archerfield Links.

> " I just had to play a course built in the 1700s – it blows my mind! "

AN AMERICAN OVERHEARD ON THE WAY TO SCOTLAND

"East Lothian is a golfers' heaven in that we have twenty-one golf courses within our small area, it really is Scotland's Golf Coast," says Gordon Simpson, the club secretary at Gullane. "As well as Muirfield, our famous neighbours and home of the Honourable Company of Edinburgh Golfers, we have other world-renowned courses such as North Berwick, and The Renaissance Club is just a stone's throw away from Gullane. We are not simply a championship venue, the area caters for all and we also have some magnificent hidden gems such as the Glen, Kilspindie and the nine-hole Gifford Golf Club. No golfer would be disappointed coming here as it is truly a magical place to play golf."

Gullane Golf Club alone is blessed with over 30,000 visiting golfers each year, the approximate split on its three courses being 8,000 on No. 1 – American Rickie Fowler won the Scottish Open there in 2015 – 12,000 on No. 2 and 10,000 on No. 3. "Our visiting golfers come from all over the world on a yearly basis to play one of our three fantastic golf courses," adds Simpson. "Visitors flock to Gullane for many reasons, but I think one of the main ones is the unique proposition that we hold. We have three courses which suit all types of golfer, young or old, good or bad, so the fact we can cater for every-one's needs is a huge asset. Also, let us

Muirfield has staged The Open on 16 occasions.

Dunbar Golf Club.

Longniddry Golf Club.

not forget that all three of the courses allow you the pleasure of playing your way up Gullane Hill – where golf has been played for more than 350 years – which unleashes the true selling point: the incredible views of the three courses as well as the many landmarks in East Lothian, Fife and Edinburgh.

"We also have two extremely different clubhouses. The main Members' Clubhouse is very traditional in style and quite grand in stature, whereas the newly refurbished Links Clubhouse is the complete opposite, very modern and bright where a more casual, relaxed family feel is to be had. So, when you put the courses, clubhouses, range and short game facilities and two pro shops together, we are more a golf destination than your traditional golf club."

SCOTLAND VS. IRELAND?

It's often been claimed that Ireland, home, in fairness, to some cracking courses, had stolen a march on Scotland in terms of golf tourism, due partly to people involved in that business perhaps having rested on their laurels and taking those visitors from around the globe for granted. Not so, according to a golf tourism expert: "That all came about on the back of the 2006 Ryder Cup in Ireland and what happened is that it backfired on them," he says. "The K Club and other venues thought they were going to be gallus and put their prices up to £300 to £400 and it backfired. Actually, Scotland is miles ahead of Ireland but the reason people keep saying 'Ireland are on the ball' or 'Ireland are doing this or that' is only because Ireland get a lot of funding from government as they are still part of the European Union and they then have bigger stands and go to more events and so on. But don't be fooled by any argument. Scotland is miles ahead of Ireland as far as golf tourism goes. If you go to the PGA Show in Orlando, the Irish stand is always bigger than the Scottish stand. People always say 'we need a bigger stand', but that's not the case. In fact, my attitude towards it is that we don't even need to go because we only need to open up our phone lines and provide an email address when people enquire as they want to come and play our courses more than they do the ones in Ireland."

Perry Golf, a company formed by brothers Colin and Gordon Dalgleish, is one of the leading providers of international golf tours and cruises to dozens of the world's most desirable destinations, with Scotland being either at the top or close to the top of the lists of their clients for good reason.

"In terms of inbound international golf tourism to Scotland, I would consider it to be rated by visitors and potential visitors very highly in terms of the quality of venues we have available to be accessed by anyone, many being world class and renowned courses including those which regularly host The Open," says Colin, a former Scottish Amateur champion who captained a Great Britain & Ireland side that contained Rory McIlroy in the 2007 Walker Cup at Royal County Down. "Beyond the biggest names, we also have an incredibly strong supporting cast of venues. The quality and condition of these venues across the board, and the welcome extended to visiting golfers, is rated very highly. Supporting the core golf product, Scotland now has a hospitality sector of hotels and restaurants and bars, and available ground transportation,

Cabot Highlands.

" We aim for Gleneagles to epitomise the
very best of Scotland. "

CONOR O'LEARY

which is also rated very highly, something which could not have been said at the infancy of Scottish Golf Tourism back in the late 1970s or early 1980s. Taken in its entirety, Scotland now has a golf tourism offering of which it can be justifiably very proud."

Not necessarily in order but the five main golfing areas in Scotland in terms of tourism are: St Andrews/Fife/Angus, East Lothian/Edinburgh, Ayrshire, Inverness/Dornoch and Aberdeen/North East. International guests typically take in two or three of those areas while the most common six- or seven-day trip would be St Andrews/Fife/Angus and Ayrshire as that offers the chance to play most of The Open venues, both past and present.

"I would say the area which has moved fastest up the 'must play and visit' list in the last 15 years is Inverness/Dornoch/Cabot Highlands/Nairn as its golf tourism and hospitality product just gets better and better," adds Dalgleish. "In addition to its transportation links improving, that's down to its overall appeal, including the great and varied on-golf tourism products it offers."

Clubhouse at Cabot Highlands.

WHERE TO STAY?

The variety of accommodation on offer to visiting golfers ticks every box. There's homely bed & breakfast places for those on a budget, lots of so-called premium hotels and, of course, luxurious locations as well. Once lacking, on-course accommodation has also become an option. The Lodge at Craigielaw, for example, is now a popular base for golfers heading to East Lothian while, over on the west coast, a mix of different-sized lodges at Dundonald Links, where each complex has been built around a course-standard putting green, were quickly snapped up for the 152nd Open at nearby Royal Troon.

"Quality accommodation in Ayrshire is limited, especially catering for golf groups of many sizes," says Lindsey Esse, managing director of Darwin Escapes, owners of the Ayrshire venue. "Adding the lodges has given a unique style of golfing accommodation to the west coast of Scotland, from a two-bedroom lodge to a six-bedroom lodge, and we attract large and small groups of golfers to enjoy both self-catering and or restaurant facilities. One night you might dine out at our facilities or a local restaurant and the next barbecuing on the patio while enjoying the Scottish tranquillity and beauty overlooking the Isle of Arran."

The Lodges at Dundonald Links.

CHAMPIONING ALL OF SCOTLAND

An important element of golf tourism in Scotland is the product, both on and off the course, being Scottish. "It's absolutely crucial," says Conor O'Leary. "We aim for Gleneagles to epitomise the very best of Scotland, and its history and character is woven into every part of the estate, from the experiences to the pursuits to the menus in our restaurants. We actively source Scottish products, and we work with Scottish brands wherever possible, championing the country's rich tapestry of cultural, historical and natural elements. Our dedicated team of around

Comrie Golf Club.

1,200 employees is arguably our greatest asset, and many of them have been here for years – we even have generations of families working here. That kind of connection with the hotel helps us retain that Scottish identity, which is particularly important for our international guests, who will have heard about the exceptional level of service and the warm, friendly staff for whom nothing is ever too much trouble."

Which is pretty much the case across the board because even the lesser-known courses value visitors, albeit in much smaller numbers than the likes of Gullane, St Andrews or Troon. Some of the venues in more isolated areas employ an "honesty box" system whereby visitors are trusted to pay a green fee due to no club employees being around at certain times of the day. "Only in Scotland," says renowned golf journalist Alistair Tait recalling his use of such a payment method. "I first encountered the honesty box system many years ago when I played Comrie Golf Club for the first time. I next experienced it at Machrie Bay Golf Club on Arran."

> I would say the area which has moved fastest up the 'must play and visit' list in the last 15 years is Inverness, Dornoch, Cabot Highlands and Nairn.

COLIN DALGLEISH

THE BUSINESS OF GOLF

Now organised by Dundee-based media and publishing company DC Thomson, Scottish Golf Tourism Week is a showcase for a wide variety of businesses to secure business from all around the world. Held for the first time in Inverness, the 2024 edition saw 90 tour operators representing a record 40 countries take part in 3,500 face-to-face appointments as itineraries were planned for golfers to visit Scotland in both 2024 and 2025.

"It really makes a difference to local suppliers," says Andy Williams, chief revenue officer at DC Thomson. "The average benefit for each business taking part is projected to be in excess of £215,000 in the three years following the event, which is just extraordinary. The economic benefit goes beyond that, and it's estimated that Scottish Golf Tourism Week contributes an estimated £3 million to the local economy, highlighting the vital role that golf tourism plays in supporting businesses and community development across Scotland."

The Scottish Golf Tourism Awards, 2023.

7

SCOTLAND'S BOOMING GOLF BUSINESS

The original drop forge hammer used in the Nicoll factory stationed outside the factory in Largoward.

Drive through the village of Largoward on the A915 heading towards St Andrews and the last building on the right is probably Scotland's best-kept secret. That's because St Andrews Golf Company Ltd, the business located there, is arguably the oldest clubmaker in the world. It's also now one of the few companies in Scotland devoted to manufacturing across the entire golf industry, a far cry from the days when clubs, balls and all sorts of attire worn on courses were made by hand in the sport's birthplace.

While it was once names like Philp, McEwan, Anderson, Morris and Forgan that were stamped on clubs, companies such as Callaway, TaylorMade, Titleist, Ping, Wilson, Mizuno and Cobra are the familiar brands in the game these days, churning out new model after new model in a bid to help players at all levels of the game either find a bit more distance or be more forgiving for blows that aren't made with the middle of the club. The quest for improving in golf is never-ending, and equipment, expensive as it might be,

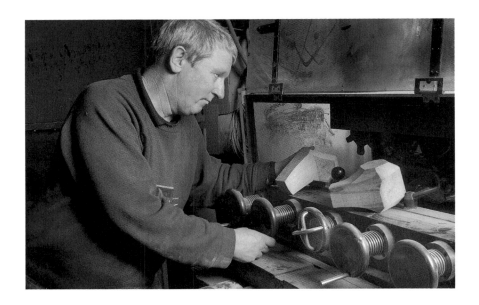

plays a vital part in that. It's refreshing, though, that deep in the heart of Fife the art of traditional golf club manufacturing is still alive, with the St Andrews Golf Company Ltd holding the Heritage Golf, George Nicoll and Tom Stewart brands while also being the official agents to Graeme Baxter, one of the world's leading golf artists.

"St Andrews Golf Company Ltd is passionate about retaining the traditions of golf club manufacture, not only in Scotland but from the 'Home of Golf' in St Andrews," says chairman Hamish Steedman. "At times, it feels a heavy responsibility to carry ourselves, particularly when challenged with escalating costs of raw materials, shipping and duties importing hickory and persimmon from overseas and, indeed, sourcing new clubmakers and apprentices interested in being trained to a required standard with the same passions. However, we are passionate about retaining the traditional clubmaking skills. The hickory game is an area of golf that is growing and we are the last company retaining these traditional manufacturing skills. In fact, with our George Nicoll brand we can demonstrate continuous manufacture

since 1881, which makes us arguably the oldest clubmaker in the world – probably Scotland's best-kept secret!"

George Nicoll started in Leven in 1881 and, by the 1950s, was one of the most successful and prolific clubmakers in the world, exporting to every country where golf was played. This was helped by the lifelong relationship it had with Sir Henry Cotton, a three-time Open winner, who endorsed the Nicoll brand all his days. Due to changes to the industry, George Nicoll closed its doors in its centenary year and was taken over by Swilken Golf in St Andrews who continued to use the Nicoll name on its clubs. When Swilken then closed its doors in 1995, Heritage Golf of St Andrews acquired its assets and trademarks, including Nicoll, Tom Stewart and St Andrews Golf Company. In 2006, when Heritage Golf were forced out of St Andrews to new premises at Largoward, the decision was made to flip the name of Heritage Golf with the dormant company of St Andrews Golf Company Ltd, which it owned. However, the George Nicoll brand and, indeed, the two clubmakers who started with Nicoll in Leven continued throughout the changes.

Ben Sayers, a highly acclaimed player himself, formed a club repair and ball-making company in 1873, starting out in what has been described as a 'lean-to shed' adjacent to the 18th tee at North Berwick Golf Club. His apprentices subsequently secured jobs around the world, though closer to home in the case of Alex Hay, who became the professional at Woburn Golf Club in Bedfordshire but is better known for his commentating partnership with Peter Alliss for the BBC. Due to the subsequent demand for the Ben Sayers brand, the business moved to a new factory in the East Lothian town in the 1930s. The factory no longer exists and it's the same with a number of other companies around Scotland, including John Letters, the company probably best known for its Golden Goose putter that was launched in 1946.

Seen here is golfer Bernard 'Ben' Sayers (1856–1924), between c.1910 and c.1915.

Scotland's Booming Golf Business   149

"I think a few things led to the decline in club manufacture in Scotland," observes Steedman. "Firstly, companies were slow to adapt to the rapidly changing marketplace, particularly with large American companies coming on the scene. Secondly, labour and raw material costs escalated and companies driven by shareholder return and profits were happy for products to be made in the Far East at the expense of losing the skills and historical knowledge built up in Scotland. And, thirdly, companies did not get the support in Scotland or the UK to allow for the investment required to keep up."

Even the R&A, the St Andrews-based governing body, is unable to provide a definitive answer about the current status of clubmaking in Scotland. "I think this is a difficult one to answer fully due to the fact that clubs sold by a company based in Scotland can be imported and sold, imported for assembly and sold, or manufactured in Scotland," says a member of its equipment team. It requires a large question mark, therefore, when speculating about whether certain companies make their own clubs in Scotland, though it is known that a number of individuals make one-off clubs and especially putters.

Wilson, the clubs used by Paul Lawrie when he won The Open Championship at Carnoustie in 1999 and also by Irishman Padraig Harrington for his three major victories, still has a factory in Irvine, where it opened in 1962 to originally build clubs for the Japanese market. At peak times, more than 350 staff worked there and today it still has 70 full-time employees, with the number increasing to over a hundred with temporary workers employed during the peak golf season.

Paul Lawrie has used Wilson clubs for most of his career.

"Last year we had a member of staff retire after 50-plus years' service and we have many staff with 35-plus years' service," says Drew Parsons, the company's key account manager for golf in the UK and Ireland. "This is built from the family environment created within Wilson and we will have had many generations of the same family work in the factory over its 60-plus years. At one time everyone knew someone who worked in Wilson as it was one of the bigger employees in the town and there was a pride to say you were part of the company. There is a real passion within the staff; they have been part of the brand during the seventies and eighties when Wilson was the major golf brand and they are proud to be part of the rejuvenated Wilson as it continues to grow to be back amongst the major players in the golf market."

How much has the manufacturing process changed over the years in the Ayrshire factory? "It is actually starting to go full swing," adds Parsons. "Initially, the factory in Ayr Road was where the clubs were manufactured and built, as production moved to the Far East we became more of a warehouse facility, hence the reason to move to a larger warehouse still within Irvine about 15 years ago. But, even when we moved, we still kept the custom-build facility going and now we are building more premium irons and clubs than ever through our production cells. Custom fitting continues to grow within the retail sector and we have been at the forefront of fitting development with the launch of our new Fit-AI fitting tool, where a consumer can be fitted for club head, lie, length shaft and flex all within five swings of a club. We now have four PGA professionals or trainees working in our custom fit production to help provide that added professional touch to our club building.

"Wilson is synonymous with Scotland and has a very loyal customer base here. With Scotland being the Home of Golf, it is apt that we would have a base in Scotland and we distribute our custom-built clubs throughout EMEA from our base in Irvine. We are proud to be one of the original golf manufacturers still producing tour-quality golf products from Scotland for over 60 years."

St Andrews Golf Company Ltd is arguably the oldest clubmaker in the world.

NEW GOLF KIDS ON THE BLOCK

GolPhin also has its global headquarters in Irvine, having been founded in more recent times by Calum McPherson, a former scratch golfer with a background in aerospace manufacturing, when he discovered that his own kids weren't keen about taking up golf at first owing to the clubs being too heavy. He duly designed and developed the world's first aerospace engineered golf clubs for kids and the business has proved a resounding success.

"When your kids tell you they don't like something that you know is good for them, you'll move mountains to solve the problem," says McPherson, who was involved in his family's club-casting foundry in Johnstone on the outskirts of Glasgow before moving into the engineering world. "This feeling of rejection got me thinking. The game I fell in love with when I was five playing pitch and putt in our local public park, maybe is no longer relevant to Gen Z and millennial kids. Light bulb moment! Make it fun, make it easier, make it relevant to kids that in today's era are more attracted to instant gratification from tech games and more engaged when it is more about team rather than individualism. So off I went to the garden shed to design a golf club for kids that made it fun, engaging and easier to hit the ball in the air from the get-go."

Having achieved that through unique features that have created a "huge sweet spot", GolPhin clubs are now distributed in the United Kingdom, Europe, the United States, Australasia and the Middle East with plans afoot for Japan, Korea and South Africa. "We are the only junior product in the world permitted to use 'The Home of Golf' on our products and that is hugely important in our marketing," admits McPherson.

Golfers on Stromness Golf Course, Orkney.

View of Edinburgh from the Braid Hills.

AN AFFORDABLE SET OF CLUBS

Caley Golf, a relatively new brand in the golf equipment market, was created by Ryan Atha, an Edinburgh-born entrepreneur. While working late at night and weekends, he developed the design and technical specifications for golf clubs that aimed to make the game more accessible to as many people as possible from a pricing point of view. "I've always had a deep interest in golf and its industry," says Atha. "Growing up, I worked at the range and retail shop at Braids Hills

Golf Centre in Edinburgh, which sparked my passion for golf brands and club technology. I went on to study marketing and later moved to London, where I worked in digital marketing, helping eCommerce brands grow through online advertising. I noticed a trend of direct-to-consumer (DTC) golf equipment companies like Sub70, Stix and Takomo, and saw a great opportunity to create my own brand.

"Inspired by Scotland's inclusive approach to golf, I aimed to make the sport more affordable. With the rising costs and complexity of buying golf clubs, driven by manufacturers pushing pseudo-technology, I wanted to challenge the status quo. We offer high-quality irons made with the same materials and technologies in the same factories as the big brands, but at half the price. I started the business in March 2019 as a side hustle, and the pandemic's boost to eCommerce and golf allowed me to go full-time. Since then, we've grown year on year. We've moved from my parents' garage to a 3PL in Glasgow, which handles our global order fulfillment with a transit time of one-to-two days. I've built an A+ team in marketing, finance, and customer support, and we're on track for our biggest year yet."

MADE-TO-MEASURE CLUBS

Club-fitting has become a big part of the modern game and Scotland is home to one of the most-respected businesses in Europe in that particular area of expertise. Scott Gourlay opened his state-of-the-art fitting centre at Swanston Golf Club on the outskirts of Edinburgh in 2019 and has two similar sites in the Netherlands and now one in England as well, having just opened it in 2024.

"That's quite a hard question," admits Gourlay of being asked when he saw the potential for such a business. "Back in my early teenage years as a player and then as a PGA pro, I could understand why clubs worked for some people, but could never understand why they didn't work for others, even with two people swapping clubs. This stayed with me and one day at Dunbar while watching a lesson taking place, I was asked about my thoughts. Instead of looking at the swing, my thoughts went straight to the player's equipment. After changing the shaft length and lie, the difference to the player's ball flight and strike changed instantly. Twenty-three years later, I still make clubs for this player."

That passion was inspired by someone who worked for the aforementioned Ben Sayers company. "I'm not sure I ever saw potential in creating a fitting business, as I was more interested in finding a solution to create a proper fitting," adds Gourlay. "Having been involved with brands at fitting events and tour events and when I was around 15 years old, I came across Jim Affleck, who had been a club builder with Ben Sayers. He inspired my passion for club building, which then allowed me to start creating a solution to the problems I saw around the fitting of golf clubs."

Since opening his main studio on the outskirts of the Scottish capital after initially being based at Craigmillar Park Golf Club, Scott Gourlay Golf Technology has gone from strength to strength. "Our latest addition is that our fitters are now able to change grips between fittings, allowing each player to test and feel how such grip texture or size will affect the club while in the fitting process. Both studios in the Netherlands are still going strong and all our studios have a major part to play within the SGGT set up. In 2024, we opened up our first new fitting studio in England at South Chesterfield Golf Club, which doubled our UK capacity and extended our reach into the Midlands and southern England."

In his own way, Gourlay is showing that Scotland can still make its mark in the game, even though the majority of the clubs these days are produced in Asia. "For us, SGGT offers a tailored custom fitting experience in each of our locations," he says. "We have several customers who come to Scotland from overseas to be fitted, so coming to the Home of Golf may be important to them. Whilst the fitting is done in many locations, all our clubs are built in-house at our Swanston workshop, so we are proud to say that they are made in and distributed from Scotland."

Swanston Golf Club.

WASTE NOT WANT NOT

Other Scottish businesses are also thriving in the golf market. Take golf-clubs4cash, for example. It started in an attic in Edinburgh but has grown into a company that now employs more than a hundred people, stocks around 60,000 golf clubs and posts hundreds of parcels every day to customers around the world.

"I turned 18 in December 2008 and had my golf clubs stolen from me just a couple of months later," said Murray Winton, the co-founder. "I then became very enthusiastic about buying and selling used golf clubs on eBay, to try and rebuild a suitable golf set and sell clubs for a profit if they didn't suit me. I built up a small amount of stock which I stored at home and, after a period of 'dabbling', I agreed to sell half my stock to one of my friends, Martin Lambert, in the summer of 2011. We then started trading as a partnership on eBay. I moved into a small house with a big attic in 2012 to allow some space for the business and, eventually, Martin and I quit our day jobs and incorporated the business in 2014.

"We then established our own website, moved into bigger premises in 2015 and converted the unit into a showroom. We still operate out of that unit today, and since then we've taken five additional units in Bilston Glen Industrial Estate to facilitate our growth. In 2022, we opened an additional store in Warrington, which has been successful, as this has helped to introduce us to golfers living south of the border and establish our brand."

DIAMONDS ARE A GOLFER'S BEST FRIEND

Lots of Scottish knitwear brands are synonymous with golf. Take Pringle of Scotland, for example. Founded in 1815 by Robert Pringle, it has been producing cashmere since 1870 and the Borders-based company's clothing was hugely popular at a time when 'Geometric George', which was originally inspired by the diamond pattern of the company's renowned Argyle knit, adorned the front of sweaters. It was worn by Nick Faldo as he landed a first win in The Open at Muirfield in 1987 before 'Geometric George' shot to fame as the Englishman then triumphed in both The Masters at Augusta National and The Open at St Andrews three years later.

Hawick-based Lyle & Scott was founded in the town in 1874 by William Lyle and Walter Scott, with Gary Player, Greg Norman and Tony Jacklin among those to sport its distinct logo after introducing a golf range in 1976. Television star Ronnie Corbett, who truly loved his golf, did as well, even wearing his Lyle & Scott jumpers when appearing on *The Two Ronnies*. After a 200-year production run, Hawick-based Peter Scott was forced to close, but business is still booming for Glenmuir, a name that is widely known around the world.

> When your kids tell you they don't like something that you know is good for them, you'll move mountains to solve the problem.

CALUM McPHERSON

Wearing a Pringle jersey, Nick Faldo shows off the Claret Jug.

Established in 1891 by Andrew MacDougall in Lanark, Glenmuir is now owned by the Ruia family, meaning it is part of the Ruia Textile Group, and employs around 85 staff at its original factory in the Clyde Valley, from where a wide range of garments, which also now include Sunderland of Scotland waterproof clothing, are distributed to 27 countries around the world. "Our Scottish identity is extremely important," says Mansi Ruia Shah, head of public relations. "It is part of our DNA, being in Scotland, the Home of Golf, our 130 years-plus Scottish heritage is something which is knitted into each thread of our products."

For the 2024 DP World Tour season, four-time winner Stephen Gallacher from Scotland and double champion on the circuit Shubhankar Sharma from India both wore Glenmuir clothing. "Being the Official Apparel Licensee for the Ryder Cup, The Open and Solheim Cup gives us a great presence at these events and allows us to engage with golf fans and for them to experience our products and understand the passion, love and care we put into each and every one," adds Ruia Shah. "Being worn by DP World Tour winners such as Stephen and Shubhankar is also a testament to the quality of the products and how they are able to perform in the various climates across the globe which form part of the tour schedule."

HICKORY HEALTH

As previously mentioned, hickory golf is an area of the game that is showing a resurgence and healthy growth, helped by events like the World Hickory Open Championship, won by two-time major champion Sandy Lyle in both 2014 and 2016, raising the profile of how the game used to be played and the participants also being dressed from a bygone era.

"A bit like vinyl or classic cars, golfers with disposable income are turning to the joys of playing with or collecting hickory," says Hamish Steedman. "As chairman of the World Hickory Open, we regularly get over 12 countries being represented in our annual tournament with people from as far away as China, Japan, Australia, North America and across Europe participating. Unfortunately, like many things, passion is stirred the further from home you are and very few people in the UK and particularly Scotland embrace the history of the game."

Some will contest that claim, but it's true that Steedman's passion for the traditions of the game and, in particular, the history of the manufacturing side of it being retained in the Home of Golf doesn't seem to be shared by others. "Justification for retaining a connection with St Andrews is seen in the visitors we get each year to our shop and factory

Golfers in the World Hickory Open
Championship at Longniddry Golf Club.

and the glowing comments of support we receive," he says. "It is disappointing in a way that this is not reflected close to home. For example, in 2006 when supermarket chain Morrisons, who were our landlords in St Andrews, gained planning permission to extend into our factory – something in the end which did not happen – our lease was terminated. Raising our concerns with the local council about keeping the last golf club manufacturer in town received little sympathy. People overseas want to be part of Scotland and its history, be it golf or otherwise, and we are very poor as a nation at exploiting that."

That, of course, is a matter of opinion, yet there can be no denying that Scotland has and always will be hugely respected in terms of any golf-related business because it's a country, quite frankly, that is viewed like no other around the world when it comes to this particular sport.

Golfers in the World Hickory Open Championships at Longniddry Golf Club.

8

SCOTLAND'S
CLUBHOUSES

**Walk into numerous clubhouses in
Scotland and you'd be forgiven for
thinking you had strayed into a museum
due to the cabinets, corridors and in
some cases even entire rooms housing
historic trophies, timelines and treasures.**
If you've got it, then flaunt it. Rightly so!
And, thus, some of the oldest golf clubs in
the world use their clubhouses to share
stories and memories that deserve to be
shared with visitors from far and wide.

Take Royal Troon, for instance. The
venue for the 152nd Open Championship
in 2024, it has had an Art and Heritage
Committee in existence since 2011.
Thanks to its contribution on behalf of the
membership, a hugely impressive display
of artefacts of historical importance in
the main corridor of the Ayrshire club's
iconic sandstone clubhouse has probably
led to many people facing a dash to the
first tee after losing track of time taking
everything in.

"Prior to the clubhouse being
upgraded in 2006, many items of historic
interest were locked away in 'safe
cupboards'," says Ronald Anderson, the
club captain. "The club at this time were
fortunate in having a group who were
passionately interested in the club's
history and heritage and had proposed
that incorporated into the 'upgrade'
would be provision for cabinets which
could display the most significant items.
It is difficult to put a time frame to the

Royal Troon Golf Club.

Muirfield, home of The Honourable Company of Edinburgh Golfers.

actual creation of the displays as the material had been collected over many years. Suffice to say that the recent upgrade to the displays was thanks to the input principally of three people, over approximately a year."

The Dickie Cross was donated by the club's first captain in 1878, the year of its formation, while another trophy

legendary Arnold Palmer, who successfully defended the Claret Jug there in The Open in 1962. Equally eye catching, an imposing one of Colin Montgomerie, who regards the club as his golfing "home" after growing up around the corner, hangs in the Ailsa Room and was painted by the award-winning Andrew Taylor.

"One of the challenges of recording – or not – items of historic interest is to do it in a manner that makes it readily accessible and visible to all, both members and visitors," adds Anderson. "The method adopted at Troon depicts the history and principal events and allows for the display to be reasonably easily updated as required. All of this is immensely important as very often the wealth of memorabilia that clubs acquire is hidden away in storage, easily overlooked and/or forgotten."

Equally fascinating when you venture through its doors is the clubhouse at Muirfield, home of the Honourable Company of Edinburgh Golfers. Heritage tours are a regular feature of club life at the East Lothian venue, with members, guests, clubhouse staff, greenkeepers and caddies having all taken the opportunity to learn more about the past, the present and plans for the future. Robin Dow conducted such tours during the club's first staging of the AIG Women's Open in 2022, with a Heritage Committee now having nine members focusing solely on such matters.

of interest is the Jenkins Trophy, which was inaugurated in 1960 and is currently presented to the club champion. JLC Jenkins was the gentleman responsible for The Open first being played at Troon in 1923, won by Englishman Arthur Havers. A fine collection of paintings, meanwhile, includes one by renowned Scottish portraitist, Anne Mackintosh, of the

The Dining Room at Muirfield.

"In 2016, the newly formed group had sufficient insight to fully appreciate that the Honourable Company has a very special place in the history and development of golf, that this had not always been prioritised in past years, that the club's own heritage is second to none and that it was a huge challenge to honour our heritage and enrich our legacy for future generations," says Dow. "This insight resulted in a recognition of the need to engage specialist external help. Members did not have the experience, deep knowledge, particular skills, nor the underlying strategy to envisage and execute a comprehensive heritage programme. The most important heritage decision, taken very early on, was to work with external experts, collaborating closely with members to help achieve a world-class outcome."

There are many treasures at Muirfield. The Dining Room, for example, is the location of a high-quality reproduction – the original is in the National Library of Scotland for safekeeping – of the 'Original Rules of Golf' from 1744, as well as the 1744 Silver Club, which was donated by Edinburgh Council and is the oldest known trophy in the world of golf. Elsewhere, there are course maps of Leith and Musselburgh, both former homes, and artefacts charting the evolution of Muirfield, scorecards from its major championships from Walter Hagen in 1929 to Phil Mickelson in 2013, golf balls ranging from 1840 featheries to 1960s Dunlops and the original ballot boxes used to give or deny support to prospective members.

"The Honourable Company focus on heritage during the past decade has massively raised awareness within the club of the many aspects of our incredible history," adds Dow. "This has been extremely positive and members are now in a position to entertain guests and engage with visitors, armed with a decent knowledge and understanding of the role our predecessors played in the development of the game of golf.

"The Honourable Company's role in the growth of The Open Championship, our part ownership of the Claret Jug, our position as one of only two clubs to host the 'full house' of The Open, The Amateur, the Ryder Cup, the Walker Cup, the Curtis Cup, the Vagliano Trophy, the Women's Open and the Senior Open are all facts that make members feel good about the club. We have so many great stories to tell and wonderful anecdotes to relate covering a huge span of history.

"We also have a golf course – one of our most important physical objects – that consistently ranks among the top courses in the world in almost every authoritative survey. Members and members of the public tend to know a good deal more about the course – Muirfield – than they do about the Honourable Company of Edinburgh Golfers. We are intent on changing the balance so that HCEG, while still a private club that guards its privacy, becomes much better known in respect of our heritage and our contribution to the evolution of golf.

"It is also the case that HCEG today is a great deal more communicative than it was in days of yore. This is a very important development, and was particularly relevant in the build-up to hosting the AIG Women's Open in 2022. The club was determined to demonstrate not only that we are the 'dedicated custodians of a celebrated links' but also that we welcome the world to our home at Muirfield. The Honourable Company proudly hosted the AIG Women's Open and literally opened our doors to engage with competitors, spectators, officials, members' guests, the media and commentators of all sorts."

> The members are both users and preservers of the Society – in a way, we are caretakers.

DONALD ROBERTSON

AIG WOMEN'S OPEN

3

370 YARDS 338 METRES PA

AIG WOMEN'S OPEN

#AIGWO

Scotland's Louise Duncan hits a tee shot in the 2022 AIG Women's Open at Muirfield.

A favourite clubhouse for many is the one at Panmure where, through a strong link to the Jute trading industry, records show that the design was loosely based on Royal Calcutta Golf Club. The centre-piece of the Angus club, celebrating its heritage, are the Silver Clubs. The original long-nosed one from 1845 was added to over the years and the Earl of Dalhousie's coat of arms is engraved on the head of each one to mark his position as the Honorary President. A list of founding members is also a coveted item while a photo of Macdonald Smith – who was born in Carnoustie before emigrating to the United States – on the 16th tee when he was playing the qualifier for the first Open Championship at Carnoustie in 1931 is always widely admired. Rightly so, Panmure trumpets its link with the great Ben Hogan, who, on his one and only visit to Scotland to play in The Open at Carnoustie in 1935, spent two weeks there accompanied only by his caddie, Cecil Timms, to acclimatise to the terrain of links golf and to acquaint himself with the smaller 1.62 inch British golf ball. It paid off as he got his hands on the Claret Jug – his final major victory.

Panmure Golf Club.

The Walker Cup Room at Kilmarnock
(Barassie) Golf Club.

"We are hugely fortunate to have the combination of the course heritage, with Old Tom Morris laying out the course in 1899, combined with our iconic clubhouse," says David Brodie, the club's general manager. "Whether it is big events or guests visiting the club, it is wonderful to see everyone enjoy spending time in the clubhouse. The connection to Mr Hogan is another great moment in the club's history and everyone enjoys the anecdotal stories of his time with us.

"It is an ongoing process, and we try to follow the template the club has previously utilised. As an example, when we hosted the R&A Girls' Amateur Championship in 2019, there was an anniversary dinner and we asked all of the past champions to sign a course flag, which is now framed and hanging in the clubhouse. We continue to search for new pieces to complement the current memorabilia."

Bathgate in West Lothian rightly celebrates having produced three Ryder Cup players in Eric Brown, Bernard Gallacher and Stephen Gallacher while, back on the Ayrshire coast, Kilmarnock (Barassie) has a room devoted to four of its members who represented Great Britain & Ireland in the Walker Cup. Jim Milligan holed the winning putt in Great Britain & Ireland's first-ever victory on US soil in that biennial bout at Peachtree in 1989 before playing again two years later at Portmarnock.

Gordon Sherry (1995 at Royal Porthcawl), Jack McDonald (2015 at Royal Lytham) and Euan Walker (2019 at Royal Liverpool) all then followed in his footsteps by facing the Americans.

"It is very important," says David Addison, the club's general manager, of the Walker Cup Players' Lounge at Kilmarnock (Brassie). "It shows that we have a strong tradition of producing great talent within the club. All of our Walker Cup players were junior members and are still members of the club. I'm not 100 per cent sure who came up with the idea for the room, but I think it was discussed by our two previous club chairs whilst at the 2019 match watching Euan Walker. Outwith this, another member, Joan Hastings, played in the 1966 Curtis Cup and many junior members have been capped for Scotland."

A full-length wall wrap of the quartet forms a feature wall in the room while various pieces of memorabilia include golf bags and clothing; in addition, there's the wedge that Milligan used to chip in as he created that slice of history in Georgia by securing a halve against the legendary American amateur, Jay Sigel, in the second-day singles. "We use the Walker Cup Players' Lounge for members and visitors to enjoy before and after golf," adds Addison. "It's a nice room overlooking the putting green and gives golfers a good feeling before their game and also afterwards."

Though relatively few people get the opportunity to see inside it, visitors from all around the world cherish the opportunity to get a photograph taken with the Royal & Ancient Golf Club of St Andrews clubhouse in the background, either in a snap from close to the first tee on the Old Course or, in most cases, standing on the Swilcan Bridge. Arguably the most famous building in golf, it recently underwent a major renovation, though that will have gone unnoticed by many due to the fact that the main work as part of the largest undertaking in a hundred years was carried out below ground level. Involving work that went down five metres – thankfully through sand rather than rock – plush new locker-rooms, including space to offer women's facilities, have been built, getting a "baptism of fire" when more than 600 members converged on St Andrews for the R&A's Spring Meeting in 2024.

The Royal & Ancient Golf Club of St Andrews.

Crail Golfing Society Clubhouse.

The improvements also include a new heritage lounge displaying historic architectural plans of the clubhouse; a new Members' Shop; a refurbished Trophy Room displaying the club's trophies and medals; and a new golf concierge desk offering services to members.

"We are pleased to have made these improvements while retaining its special character and appearance," says Martin Slumbers, secretary of the Royal & Ancient Golf Club of St Andrews at the time of the clubhouse reopening in April 2024. "All members will now be able to enjoy the use of new and improved facilities which will enrich their experience of visiting and playing golf in St Andrews."

Crail Golfing Society, which sits just along the coast towards the East Neuk of Fife, makes the most of its being the seventh oldest golf club in the world. It immediately grabs the attention of visitors before they enter the main lounge in a clubhouse that sits high above the Balcomie Links, the oldest of its two courses. "When we were redoing the clubhouse in 2006, the architect asked 'What's the most important thing to your club?'" recalls David Roy, the club manager. "And the reply was the seaside and the history. So, when he redesigned the clubhouse, the first thing you see is the sea and when you walk inside you are surrounded by the club's history. It was specifically designed that way and it works."

Mainly through bequeathments from members over the years, the club has built up an impressive collection of objects. "We've got some really interesting artefacts, as lots of clubhouses have," adds Roy, who admits to being passionate about heritage and history himself. "There's two things that I point out to people who are interested. There's the Lindsay Medal, which once made an appearance on the BBC's *Antiques Roadshow* when it visited St Andrews. It was donated to the club by Lord Lindsay for an Open competition, which was the world's first such event as it pre-dates The Open Championship by almost 30 years. Bob Kirk, Davie Anderson, Alan Robertson and all the other top players

at that time came down and played in it. Alan Robertson eventually won but, when that happened, that's when the club changed the rules and made it a closed competition. Typical club thing to do [laughing]. We think that's the only trophy Alan Robertson ever won in his life. It's the club's oldest trophy and also probably the most valuable one.

"We've also got an Old Tom Morris club. That was the club he used to officially reopen Balcomie after he did the redesign in 1895. Then, of course, there's the Ranken Todd Bowl, which is a punch-bowl; that's what they used to drink back then and, by all accounts, it was a fairly noxious, potent punch. The oddest thing we've got – and it's above my head in the office – is a single bedpost from a four-poster bed from the first captain, William Ranken!"

A favourite clubhouse for many is the one at Panmure.

The Barnton Bell – which used to be rung before the train heading to Edinburgh left the nearby but now closed Barnton station – and the Rhind Stone, which depicts in bas-relief two golfers and their caddies at one of the greens on Bruntsfield Links with Edinburgh Castle in the background, are part of the clubhouse heritage at Royal Burgess Golfing Society. "We believe that the members are both users and preservers of the Society – in a way, we are caretakers," says Donald Robertson, the club's archivist.

The Royal Burgess Golfing Society.

A MODERN TOUCH

While lots of people love feeling a part of history, and that is the case in clubhouses all around the country, others prefer something modern when it comes to clubhouse comforts. Numerous clubs offer facilities that tick that particular box. The clubhouses at Kingsbarns Golf Links and Cabot Highlands (better known as Castle Stuart) both have a homely feel while the one at Dumbarnie Links has been designed to be functional, welcoming and entertaining.

"None of the areas in our clubhouse could be described as opulent or of over-generous proportions," says David Scott, the general manager at the Fife venue. "This was deliberate: our lounge can hold only 72 guests and so is smaller than many other venues, but we have created a vibe that is equal to some of the best in Scotland. A 25-foot bar with four large TV screens showing sports and music coming through our Sonos system sets the tone for the room. In front of our large lounge windows, we have a long south-facing patio area and so, on warmer days, we find many of our guests sitting outside and taking in the wonderful views down our first hole, across the Firth of Forth and over to East Lothian.

Kingsbarns Golf Links.

We consistently hear from tour operators, golfers and our own team, how much fun our guests are having and how anti-stuffy it is, which is music to my ears! Taking the entertainment and fun from the clubhouse to the golf course, our starter enjoys pouring a wee dram of whisky on our first tee. We believe we are the only club in Scotland that has this offering to golfers."

After it opened in 2003, visitors to Dundonald Links used what was often described as the "nicest Portakabin you'll ever come across" for its clubhouse, before a permanent facility was built after the Ayrshire venue was bought by Darwin Escapes from Loch Lomond Golf Club in 2019. It's been positioned so that panoramic views across not only the golf course but also over to Arran in the west can be enjoyed from the restaurant, bar and outside patio on the first floor. Oh, and the old golf clubs in circles on the ceiling are there to give a nod to the history of the great game.

"I wanted an old feel with a modern take in areas like the pro shop and changing rooms by using a dark wenge wood with modern local artwork, colours, textures and rugs," says Lindsey Esse, managing director of Darwin Escapes. "A steam room and sauna in each changing room gives the golfer a true feeling of relaxation after a round of golf while the Bothy, our halfway house, was a key introduction. The fire is on in the winter for a hot soup and a pie – it's given us a real halfway house destination."

Add in the all-important staff members – club professionals, club caterers, club secretaries and managers, starters and so on – and the clubhouses certainly add to the culture of golf in Scotland, even though the courses they sit on are the star attractions.

Dundonald Links.

9

SCOTLAND'S CADDIES AND GREENKEEPERS

Damian Moore on caddying duties in the 2014 Ryder Cup.

WITH A CADDIE AT HAND

The courses may be the main attraction for golfers visiting Scotland but playing them with a caddie at your side enhances the experience. "Imagine driving an Aston Martin and you tried to put diesel in the engine instead of petrol," says Damian Moore, an Englishman who now lives in Scotland and combines his caddying career on professional tours with picking up bags at Muirfield when he's at home in Gullane. "That's what it would be like if you didn't take a caddie on a top Scottish course – the two go hand in hand!"

All the top courses in the country now offer a caddying service and, though it may not be used too often by Scots themselves, that's only because they are familiar with the humps, bumps, breaks and borrows. For visitors, in contrast, it's extremely helpful to have someone offering various snippets of advice that can make a special day even more rewarding. With that in mind, and to cater for the ever-growing number of golfers heading

to the country, the number of caddies in Scotland is now enough to form a small army.

In St Andrews, where around 33,000 caddie rounds are clocked up per year across the Links Trust courses, approximately 200 caddies are on the books during the high season. If there's one course in the world where a caddie is recommended to ensure you get as much satisfaction as possible out of a round, then it is probably the Old Course, venue for The Open on a record 30 occasions, most recently for the 150th edition in 2022.

"The Old Course is a very unique course, with no obvious lines off the tees and most of the hazards hidden from view," says Nick Robertson, one of the most experienced loopers on that Links Trust list. "The course has massive greens, with two flags on seven of them – and the flags can be a hundred yards apart! Hard to get your head round that, even with all the up-to-date technology. So, if you are playing the Old Course for the first time, a caddie is essential."

Rodney Soutar, who has caddied at Carnoustie for more than 40 years, echoes that view in the case of the Angus venue, another of the courses used by the R&A for The Open, AIG Women's Open and the Senior Open. "For some, it's a one-off experience they will never forget," he says. "Golf is the only sport in the world where you can basically be a professional for the day. You can't go to Wimbledon, Hampden or Wembley and play either tennis or football, but, with golf, you are walking the fairways where the greats have walked and played – Ben Hogan, Jack Nicklaus, Gary Player, Tom Watson, Seve Ballesteros, Tiger Woods and so on. And, as you do so, you'll have a man or woman on the bag discussing yardages and shots, reading putts, cleaning clubs and golf balls."

It's not often in life that you meet someone for the first time and then immediately spend four or five hours in their company, but it happens all the time when it comes to golfers and caddies and, through that connection, life-long friendships have been struck and, equally

significantly, advice and help offered the other way round. "You meet so many different and interesting people from all walks of life and, after four or five hours in their company, you end up getting to know the guests pretty well," admits Rob Thorp, the caddiemaster at Dumbarnie Links. "You can also end up forming strong friendships with guests as they return year after year. Additionally, you get paid to enhance people's experiences, which I see as a hugely rewarding role."

Moore, who caddied for Stephen Gallacher when he pulled off back-to-back wins in the Dubai Desert Classic, the "Middle East Major" on the DP World Tour, in 2013 and 2014, concurs. "One of the amazing things about caddying is you never know who you might meet and

Once a caddie has earned the trust of their player, they start opening up and tell their life stories.

that's what I tell my son," he declares. "In the five hours you spend guiding folks around a golf course, you can start friendships for life. Someone can take a shine to you and who knows where it might go."

Soutar reckons caddies can get the same kick out of being on someone's bag on a certain day as the person they are helping. "You get to meet people from all walks of life, some people you wouldn't get near to on a normal day," he adds. "For instance, Neil Armstrong, Michael Douglas, Hugh Grant, Seve, Tiger. Yet, you can be out there for five hours at a time with them. Some of the young caddies here have also been pointed in the right direction regarding scholarships. A pleasing factor for me is seeing the 16 to 18-year-olds turning into adults through caddying, just by meeting people and working with adults, which helps them find their own way in life through college, university and so on."

Gordon Milligan started caddying at Muirfield after he was made redundant in 1999. "My highlight was caddying for a young Irish golfer in the Home

A young Shane Lowry.

Internationals in 2008," he recalls. "I thought I was going to get sacked when I took nine yards off from a sprinkler head – no rangefinders were allowed in those days – instead of adding it on. He hit a great shot down the stick and it came up well short. I owned up and he said, 'Let that be your last mistake,' and it was, thank God. I knew then that this guy was good and he had one of the finest touches round the green I had witnessed. That year Ireland won the Home Internationals and my golfer went on to win the Irish Open the following year as an amateur and then The Open Championship at Royal Portrush in 2019. He had a huge personality and that was my first introduction to Shane Lowry!"

Most Scottish caddies are golfers themselves, meaning they are well versed in the dos and don'ts in the sport. They know their respective courses like the back of their hand and, though it may be difficult at times to be convinced when they pick out targets from tees and lines on greens, it definitely pays to heed any advice they offer during a round.

"The majority of our caddies come with experience from other venues, so training requirements are fairly light touch other than some course specific elements, including course history, which always goes down well with golfers. Often it's the historical stories they remember more than the golfing advice," says John Grant, the director of golf at St Andrews Links Trust. "When we take on newer and younger caddies, they'll go through a short internal training programme covering golf etiquette and course information with our caddie team before they are paired with customers. Our seasoned caddies are usually great with the less experienced ones, helping them through various things on the course, taking them under their wings and giving advice where required."

Once a caddie has earned the trust of their player, they start opening up and will often tell their life stories. On some occasions, though, introductions don't need to be made. Nick Robertson, for instance, turned up at St Andrews one day to find out he'd been handed the enjoyable task of caddying for the former US President Bill Clinton. During the course of that round, he happily recalls one of his favourite stories from the profession. "He decided to go to the WC at the Halfway House," says Robertson, whose son, Graeme, won the Loch Lomond Whiskies Scottish PGA Championship in 2023 and 2024, when he also qualified for The Open at Royal Liverpool. "When the president was inside, his burly bodyguards took station either side of the entrance. I happened to mention that there was another door to the rear of the building. Blind panic ensued as the bodyguards rushed to the other entrance!"

He also chuckles about being out on the Old Course one day with a group of four Japanese players. "One of the guys asked about a small stone in the middle of the fifth fairway," he says. "This stone is an old boundary dating back to when the course was first made. It looks very much like a small stone tombstone. So, as a bit of devilment I said, 'Oh that is where my father is buried!' The four gentlemen lined up and reverently bowed in respect."

When Soutar started out, caddies carried two bags and, unlike today, there were no yardage books containing all sorts of numbers. "Eye-balled was the done thing back then," he recalls. One of his favourite stories is about an American who'd found the Barry Burn on numerous occasions in his round at Carnoustie. It, of course, was made famous by Jean van de Velde during The Open in 1999, when the Frenchman took off his socks and shoes to ponder the possibility of playing a shot out of it during a calamitous final hole. "He was taking his clubs to the car park and said to his caddie, 'I'm going back to St Andrews, how do I get back?' The caddie said, 'Go to the top of the road and turn right, you'll head out of Carnoustie and see a sign post for Forfar, head there and take A90 to Dundee and go over Tay Bridge to St Andrews.' The American said, 'Is that not a long way?' To which he replied, 'Yes, but you won't have to cross the Barry Burn again!'"

Rob Thorp worked at St Andrews before taking up his role at Dumbarnie Links, where a total of 140 caddies are licensed in the high season – June, July and August – and are selected from a pool of around two hundred. In 2023, the busiest day saw 164 jobs being covered, with between 35 and 40 caddies often doing two rounds in a day. He was doing a double shift himself one day on the Old

He turns up one day to find out he'd been handed the enjoyable task of caddying for Bill Clinton.

The Old Course at St Andrews.

Students at The Elmwood Campus of Scotland's Rural College (SRUC).

Course when he experienced his funniest moment in the job.

"A fellow caddie – let's call him Dave – had his guest's bag on a push cart due to the size and weight of it. Anyone planning a trip to Scotland and intending on asking caddies to carry, please bring a lightweight carry bag," he says. "Dave's golfer hit his second shot and came up short in the burn, to which Dave received verbals about the accuracy of the yardage provided. When they got to the Swilcan Burn, Dave went to fetch the ball retriever to fish his guy's ball out. However, he

forgot to put the wheel brake on the cart and while his back was turned, his golfer's bag and cart rolled straight into the burn. Due to previous rainfall the water level was quite high and the bag was submerged.

"Dave's reactions were second to none and he jumped straight in after it, hauled it out onto the side of the burn and swiftly threw the cart out after it. When he got out, he tipped the bag upside down to empty the water. Meanwhile, myself and the other caddies in the group were roaring with laughter.

Dave's golfer was not amused. In fact, he was hacked off and became very, very quiet for the remainder of the round. We quietly ribbed Dave at every tee box thereafter, asking if his guest's grips were dry yet? Or how come his golfer had soaking wet waterproofs when it hadn't rained that day. I still remind him about that to this day."

It's definitely hugely satisfying for caddies to hand their player a club and see them hit a good shot or pick a line on undulating greens and see the ball disappear into the hole. There are also times, though, when it's the golfer who does something that makes this particular job so satisfying.

"One of the most touching things that happened to me out there, and this to me sums up the game and the Americans' love Ben Hogan, is when I had a guy who came across from the States to play and he brought some of his late father's ashes," recalls Soutar. "He said his dad was a great Hogan fan and, having played Carnoustie himself once before, one of his dying wishes was to have them sprinkled on Hogan's Alley, the sixth hole which was named after him as he birdied it every round in 1953 when winning The Open. When my player got there, he got his picture taken by the Ben Hogan plaque and I left him to do what he had to do. He was emotional walking up the fairway before steadying himself and then proceeded to birdie it. He looked up to the heavens and the tears flowed. I have caddied in tournaments, including The Open, but that was probably the biggest buzz I've had out there. That day, to me, just summed up the beauty of the game and the job."

> Imagine driving an Aston Martin and you tried to put diesel in the engine instead of petrol – that's what it's like without a caddie on a Scottish course!

DAMIAN MOORE

MAINTAINING HIGH STANDARDS

The unsung heroes when it comes to jobs in Scottish golf are the greenkeepers. Historic as so many courses may be, they need to be in tip-top condition to satisfy club members. Equally important, visitors who have become accustomed to seeing standards rise at courses all around the world and, quite rightly, expect to be playing on well-maintained courses in this country.

Walter Woods, the long-time links superintendent at St Andrews Links Trust, was one of the true greats of the greenkeeping profession in modern times. He was instrumental in the formation of the British and International Golf Greenkeepers Association (BIGGA) in 1987 through an amalgamation of the British Golf Greenkeepers Association, the English and International Golf Greenkeepers Association and the Scottish and International Golf Greenkeepers Association. In short, his vision to modernise the industry laid down the foundation for the profession as it is today. Elmwood College, which is located close to St Andrews, is internationally renowned, having been at the forefront of greenkeeping and course management qualifications for the past quarter century or so.

The Elmwood Campus of Scotland's Rural College (SRUC).

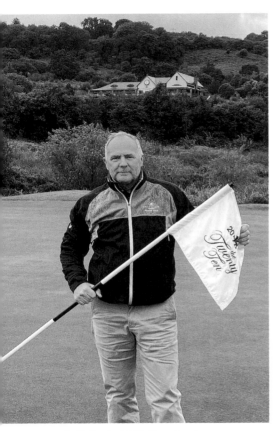

Jim McKenzie at Celtic Manor Resort.

"It's hard to find a course that's not in good nick nowadays as they are all really well maintained," says David Roy, who is now the club manager at Crail Golfing Society but began his career in golf out on the course as opposed to in an office. "But I'm a dinosaur as I started green-keeping when it hadn't really changed since before the First World War. Literally the only thing that had changed was that we were using a tractor rather than a horse. We had one set of gangs that would cut the fairways and then the semi rough and you'd just raise the height. You'd also have a couple of hand mowers and a fly mower and that was it for the whole golf course.

"To put it into perspective, when Crail bought the club from the council in 1972, they did an evaluation of the equipment in the lifeboat house, where it was stored, and it was valued at £1,500. Multiply that by twenty to take account of inflation, nowadays that wouldn't even buy you one single greens mower and we've now got over a million pounds' worth of equip-ment that we use to cut the grass."

Greenkeepers on Old Course at St Andrews.

Craig Boath, head of sustainability at Carnoustie Golf Links.

Jim McKenzie started his greenkeeping career at Haggs Castle in Glasgow then had spells at both Cawder and Renfew before moving south of the Border. He worked under fellow Scot Chris Kennedy at Wentworth, home of the DP World Tour's BMW PGA Championship, before heading along the M4 to Celtic Manor, where, in his role as the director of golf courses, he was in charge of the greenkeeping team, which included two of his compatriots as head greenkeepers for the 2010 Ryder Cup at the Newport venue.

"Since the great Donald Ross, born in Dornoch, blazed a trail across the world, there has been an admiration for Scottish greenkeepers, which has never wavered," says McKenzie. "Many golf courses around the world have either been designed, built or indeed maintained by Scotsmen. From a personal point of view, many of my contemporaries from my greenkeeping college days are either abroad working or have been in the past. A few years ago, the links superintendent at St Andrews, Walter Woods, received the Old Tom Morris Award from the Golf Course Superintendents Association of America, which was an indication of the respect for Scottish greenkeepers. Several years ago, my close friend at The Belfry introduced me to the group director of golf for the American company who owned it. I remember him telling me that the owners were so excited to have a man called Angus Macleod in charge at The Belfry – they just loved the Scottish connection."

Craig Boath has been on the greenkeeping staff at Carnoustie Golf Links for nearly 30 years, working under the legendary John Philp before being promoted to the post of links superintendent in 2019 before then becoming head of sustainability in 2022. "I have been lucky to work at a high-end golf course throughout my career," he says. "It has been an honour and a privilege to prepare the course for some of the best names in golf at the finest championships that we have hosted [including The Open, AIG Women's Open, The Senior Open and Amateur Championship].

Greenkeeper out on Carnoustie Golf Links

"As a greenkeeper, you have great pride in showing your course off to those millions that watch on TV, but, for the everyday golfer, you want to provide them with that quality that the top pros play, too. For someone coming to play Carnoustie, it could be a bucket-list trip and something that they have always dreamed of. We want to create that special moment and give them an experience they will never forget. Greenkeeping has changed over the years and, with the help of data and technology, we are able to deliver the product day after day. What is even more rewarding are the comments received post-round on how the course played, knowing that you helped give them a fantastic experience."

In his career, which took a twist after he offered to become both the head greenkeeper and part-time secretary at Linlithgow, Roy has experienced both working outdoors and indoors. "When it's nice and sunny, I miss the greenkeeping. But, when it's February and there's snow coming in from Siberia, I don't miss it at all," he declares, laughing.

Watering work at St Andrews.

10

GOLF IN SCOTLAND — A GLORIOUS FUTURE

1st hole Callander Golf Club.

Colin Montgomerie.

Even when it comes to golf, the sport Scotland gave to the world, pessimism, criticism and some negativity is often prevalent among those who either hit a wee white ball themselves for fun or are keen observers of the game. "Our top players should be doing better on the game's biggest stages" has been a common groan at times. The next generation of young talent not receiving the same level of support as other countries is another well-versed gripe. Oh, and we don't shout from the rooftops nearly as much as we should about what a fantastic country it is when it comes to the Royal & Ancient game.

"We do tend to sit on our laurels knowing we are the Home of Golf, but competition is strong, not just from within the UK but around the world," says Colin Montgomerie, one of Scotland's greatest golfing ambassadors. "We should be promoting Scottish golf in a much more positive way. People always mention the weather in Scotland before the golf but, having played the majority of my golf in the USA over the past ten years, the amount of days lost due to inclement weather there outnumbers Scotland ten to one!"

Richie Ramsay.

Stephen Gallacher and Richie Ramsay, two other players to enjoy glittering amateur careers wearing Scotland colours before going on to become successful professionals at the top level, also believe the country could do more to show itself off to the world. "As a Scot, I don't think we do golf justice," says Gallacher. "We are the Home of Golf and should be shouting it from the rooftops. There's so many great courses you could play and, in my opinion, other countries market golf much better."

"I think we can underplay what we have to offer," adds Richie Ramsay, who won the US Amateur Championship at Hazeltine in Minnesota in 2006. "Not so much with the better-known places like North Berwick, Muirfield and St Andrews. It's all the great places like the islands – Harris and Askernish, for example – and other places like Golspie, Tarland, Carrbridge. They are integral places. Also, the nine-holer at Traigh. I don't think we make the most of them and showcase that kind of original, non-commercialised community feel that is generally built into the towns and where people get a lot of enjoyment from playing them."

AN ENGLISHMAN ABROAD

It could be argued, of course, that Scots themselves aren't the best people to deliver the verdict that actually matters in terms of what the country has to offer and how that offering is viewed around the world. That's perhaps better coming from someone who wasn't born here but has witnessed, through working in golf in its birthplace, the importance of the game in Scotland.

"I have always had a fondness for golf in Scotland and enjoyed visiting to play and to attend championships," says Martin Slumbers, an Englishman who moved north of the border to succeed Peter Dawson as the R&A's CEO in 2015 and earned widespread praise in that high-profile role with the St Andrews-based governing body.

"I vividly remember attending The Open in 1984 and being mesmerised by Seve Ballesteros and the way he played golf. I had never seen anything like it before. That championship was so memorable in many ways and it cemented my appreciation for St Andrews. It is the place where it all began 600 years ago

The R&A CEO Martin Slumbers.

and it has left an indelible mark on the game. The genius and remarkable longevity of the Old Course, the public ethos of the links and the association with so many of the greatest players ever to lift a golf club combine to make it an incredibly special place.

"I would never have believed then that one day I would find myself working in St Andrews and living nearby, but that's exactly what happened. When I arrived at the R&A, I quickly realised that golf is a way of life in St Andrews and in Scotland. Almost everyone has some personal or family connection with the game and for hundreds of years it has been a game for the people. That openness remains at the heart of the town and the seven public courses mean that anyone can play whatever their level of ability. You only have to see golfers with bags slung over their shoulders as they walk around town or notice the golf bags left outside hotels and restaurants to realise that golf is in St Andrews' DNA.

"Not everywhere is as fortunate as St Andrews in terms of having so many courses, but throughout Scotland there is a tradition of public golf which has been a pathway into the game for so many golfers over the years. Some of these courses are coming under threat due to the pressure on local authority finances, but it is vital that publicly accessible courses are retained as far as possible. Golf in Scotland has a tradition of openness, accessibility and inclusiveness and, for me, that's the secret ingredient that makes it unique. It is the model that inspired the creation of the Golf It! facility in Glasgow."

Three women playing golf in Lochcarron, Wester Ross.

" I didn't really pick golf. Golf picked me from
where I lived. I lived on a golf course. "

ROBERT MACINTYRE

BRIGHTER THAN EVER?

In 2024 alone, threats to the courses at Dalmuir in Clydebank and Hollandbush near Motherwell, as well as two courses at Caird Park in Dundee, were lifted. Inevitably, others will be on council chopping blocks in years to come, but, with the R&A playing a lead role in trying to keep growing the game and Scottish Golf doing likewise, the overall future of the game in the cradle of its birthplace looks not just bright but perhaps brighter than ever.

"I think there are plenty of reasons for optimism when it comes to golf in Scotland," adds Slumbers. "There is more being done now to drive the game forward than ever before. The R&A is the only global sport governing body based in Scotland and we work closely with Scottish Golf, the national association for the game in this country. Participation rates were trending upward prior to the Covid pandemic and we have seen that accelerate since then. Golf benefited from the realisation that people could go out and play it safely while enjoying being out in nature, taking part in physical exercise and experiencing the mental health benefits of getting away from work while socialising with family and friends.

"In 2022, there were something like 210,000 registered golfers and 966,000 nine and 18-hole registered and independent golfers in Scotland (figures from the R&A's 2023 Global Golf Participation Report). If you consider that that represents almost 20 per cent of the population, then you realise how important golf is to the country. Through projects such as Golf.Golf – where people can go online and be matched up with a golf club in their area where they can go and play and receive lessons – and Golf It!, a community and family golf facility in Glasgow, we are supporting the golf industry in providing pathways into the game for newcomers of all ages.

Dalmuir Municipal Golf Course, 1958 (top) and 2006 (bottom).

Gemma Dryburgh made her LGPA Tour breakthrough in Japan in 2022.

"The strength of golf in Scotland is also evident in the number of world-class championships taking place here on a regular basis. Whether it is major championships such as The Open, the Senior Open presented by Rolex and the AIG Women's Open all taking place in Scotland in 2024 or regular staging of professional tour events in the men's and women's games, the country has a proven track record of successfully hosting events. The Scottish fans are among the most knowledgeable in the world and the top men's and women's players love playing in front of them as they test themselves on some of the game's best links and inland golf courses."

As mentioned more than once in this book, Scottish successes in the game around the world are still as important, if not more so, nowadays as at any other time in the sport's history. It was a monumental achievement, for example, when Gemma Dryburgh landed a breakthrough win on the LPGA Tour in the 2022 TOTO Japan Classic and it was exactly the same when Robert MacIntyre claimed both the RBC Canadian Open and Genesis Scottish

Robert MacIntyre had dad Dougie caddying for him when he won the RBC Canadian Open in 2024.

Open titles on the PGA Tour in 2024. To put those respective victories into perspective, Dryburgh was only the fourth player flying a Saltire to taste success on the LPGA Tour and the first since 2011, while MacIntyre, who had his dad, Dougie, caddying for him in Canada, was just the fifth player to land a tartan triumph on the PGA Tour and the first since 2020.

Dream big is MacIntyre's message to fellow Scots. "The amount of people I have spoken to, kids that I have spoken to, who have been told 'don't chase

that dream, you'll never do it, you won't achieve that'. I'd say that is Scottish-wide," says the Oban man. "It is easier to achieve it or you have more of a chance to achieve it if you are from certain areas of the country. Fact. It doesn't matter the sport. From the local areas, outside of the big cities, it is harder to make something happen just with support and funding. I was lucky I had a family that supported me from the start. My dad is sporty and knew the ability I had within other sports. I didn't really pick golf. Golf picked me

Robert MacIntyre holds aloft the Genesis Scottish Open trophy after his win at The Renaissance Club in 2024.

Rising star Hannah Darling.

from where I lived. I lived on a golf course. I have just started my journey, but I want to do something that can show people that it doesn't matter where the hell you are from, you can do what you want so long as you have the right support and the right commitment to what you are doing."

Also speaking from the heart, Gemma Dryburgh adds: "It has meant the world to me to fly the Saltire all over the world and my goal is to always represent Scotland as well as I can. I take great pride in being the sole Scot on the LPGA at the moment. I think when we all have success it really inspires everyone else to keep working hard. Playing in the Solheim Cup in 2023 and seeing the Scottish flag flying among the other countries on the team was a major career highlight. I hope to keep it flying proudly for the remainder of my career."

As was the case with both Dryburgh and MacIntyre, lots of young Scots head across the Atlantic on golf scholarships, while others are happy to stay at home and see their games develop through being part of excellent programmes at the likes of the University of Stirling and the University of St Andrews. One of those flying the Saltire with pride on the ultra-competitive US college circuit has been Hannah Darling. A member of Broomieknowe on the outskirts of Edinburgh, she won the inaugural R&A Under-16 Girls' Amateur Championship in 2018 before adding the R&A Girls' Amateur Championship three years later. She then created history along with Louise Duncan by becoming the first Scots to tee up in the Augusta National Women's Amateur in 2022.

"I have no greater pride than flying the Saltire when I play around the world," says Darling, who earned star status in her spell at the University of South Carolina playing for the Gamecocks. "I have had a number of amazing experiences so far in golf and doing so whilst representing Scotland is very special. There is no better feeling than looking up at a scoreboard and seeing the Saltire next to my name, that is the most pride I could ever feel. One event that comes to mind is playing in the Augusta National Women's Amateur. Myself and Louise were the first Scots to play the event, which was a great honour for both of us. In playing in an event like this, I hope that it inspires other Scots to feel like they can play in these events too, and have confidence in doing so having seen me do it before them.

"Since I won my first national title, in the Scottish Girls' Championship at Scotscraig in 2017, I feel I have been able to represent Scottish golf and I hope that I have given back as much as I can. The opportunities I have been given have enabled me to go on to play for Great

It's the game Scotland shared with the rest of the world.

Britain & Ireland in the Curtis Cup, along with many other events that I am more than grateful for.

"Additionally, it has meant that I have found my new home in South Carolina where I attend university as part of the golf team. It is not Scotland and, therefore, it will never be home. However, the Saltire hanging on the wall in my apartment helps with that feeling."

Which is music to the ears, of course, for Scottish Golf, with the governing body having provided Darling with both playing and coaching opportunities as she started to show promise. "It is right that we invest a significant amount of time and effort into our national squads," says CEO Robbie Clyde of the organisation often criticised for supporting elite golfers but seemingly doing little for their club counterparts. "Their success is a key priority, and players tell us that being selected to play for Scotland is a source of great pride.

"A core part of our work is supporting and developing aspiring Scottish talent, providing them with opportunities to play against the best in the world, and flying the flag for the Home of Golf. We all want Scotland to produce more Robert MacIntyres and Gemma Dryburghs, and investing in the amateur pathway is a key part of ensuring more success at pro level. The value of high-profile Scottish players on the international stage is

Picturesque Aberdour Golf Club, the author's home club.

incalculable in terms of raising awareness of the sport and encouraging partici- pation. In addition, seeing the Saltire travelling the world, contributing to the reputation and esteem of Scotland as the top place to play golf, has incredible symbolic and monetary value to the sport and to Scottish golf tourism."

Even some of the best golfers Scotland has produced over the past few decades have a "bucket list" when it comes to either courses they want to play or areas they want to tick off from a golfing perspective in their home country.

"I would like to go to the very north of Scotland and the isles and experience golf in a very different environment," admits Montgomerie. Concurring, 1999 Open champion and two-time Ryder Cup player Paul Lawrie says: "[My wife] Marian and I did the North Coast 500 last year in the car, which we absolutely loved.

And, having seen Durness, which is the most northerly course on the mainland in Britain but not having the clubs with me on that occasion, I'd love to go back up there and have a game to say I've played the most northerly course in Britain."

For Catriona Matthew it's a trip to the Ayrshire coast. "Probably Trump Turnberry as I've not played it since the changes have been made," she says, referring to changes made to the Ailsa Course by the renowned golf architect, Martin Ebert, in close conjunction with the resort's owner, Donald Trump, "so I'd love to play there."

Gallacher says Tain, Golspie, Brora, Durness and Askernish are on his list, with Ramsay's being along similar lines. "All those rugged, untouched courses where the water is crystal blue," he says. "Gems that are hidden away and a little bit hard to get to but have a rawness and beauty that is unparalleled in Scotland."

> I have no greater pride than flying the Saltire when I play around the world.

HANNAH DARLING

Gleneagles (top) and Prestwick St Nicholas Golf Club (bottom).

Royal Troon staged the 152nd Open in 2024.

Ailsa Course at Trump Turnberry.

For many, golf is the greatest sport in the world. It's the game Scotland shared with the rest of the world through pioneers who crossed the Atlantic and, nowadays, you are more than likely to find a Scot working in some capacity at countless clubs around the globe. Our expertise, the art of Scottish golf, is like a badge of honour while, on home soil, the majority of Scots know themselves how lucky they are to be out there swinging a golf club, enjoying great scenery and breathing in clean air – albeit bracing at times – on courses that, as a collection, are, quite frankly, second to none. "We are absolutely guilty of under-playing what we have in Scotland, but there's no surprise there," says David Scott, the

general manager at the highly acclaimed Dumbarnie Links in Fife. "We are a very humble nation, and we like to let our 'courses do the talking' as opposed to letting our 'clubs do the talking'."

I sincerely hope by now that you appreciate how special golf really is in Scotland and also what it means to so many people to be involved in the game and to feel as though they are not only custodians but also have a duty to pass on that role to the future generations. As the likes of Montgomerie, Matthew, Lawrie, MacIntyre and Dryburgh will testify, there's nothing that beats seeing a Saltire at the top of leaderboards on the game's biggest stages. At the same time, others get similar satisfaction from

simply being involved in the game in its birthplace and, take it from me, that is most certainly the case when it comes to writing about Scottish golf and Scottish golfers.

Doing so has allowed me to gain valuable friendships and I'm going to give the last word in this book to someone I love knowing, along with his parents, too.

"I've always been a very proud Scotsman," says Sam Torrance, a Ryder Cup legend. "I love Scotland and always have done. I went to Manchester when I was five and came back when I was nine or ten and played all my golf in Largs at Routenburn and the odd time at Kelburn. I just loved playing golf and dreamed it would be my living. I signed for John Letters and turned pro in 1972 and that was me. It was a huge thrill to play for Scotland in both the Dunhill Cup and the World Cup. I've had a wonderful relationship with fans worldwide but especially in Scotland. Even today, I was walking through Glasgow airport on a visit home and had people shouting my name. How they recognise me at 70 is unbelievable, but it's a wonderful feeling."

Wonderful indeed, and that's golf in Scotland for you!

Spectators enjoy sunshine at St Andrews.

Shiskine Golf Club.

ABOUT THE AUTHOR

Martin Dempster is a proud Borders man who is equally proud to now live in Fife. He is the golf correspondent for the *Scotsman*, *Scotland on Sunday* and *Edinburgh Evening News*. A member of the Association of Golf Writers since 1997, he served as the organisation's chairman from 2019-2023. Golf has always been one of his main passions, having cut his teeth in the sport at Eyemouth and also played at Dunbar before becoming a member of Aberdour. *The Art of Scottish Golf* is Martin's first book.

𝕏 @DempsterMartin

ACKNOWLEDGEMENTS

First and foremost, thanks to Black & White Publishing for approaching me to work on the project of my dreams and a first opportunity to spread my wings by adding a book to the hundreds and thousands of words I've written about Scottish golf and Scottish golfers over the years.

To Ali McBride for that initial approach and also to Campbell Brown, Tonje Hefte and Thomas Ross for their help and expertise in delivering what is a great-looking book.

Thanks also to every single person across the golf industry who contributed in some way. I was truly overwhelmed by both the instant and positive reaction from people after contacting them and I will be forever grateful for that as the stories they had to tell are the basis of this book.

I feel blessed to have come across an incredible group of people through covering golf and, in particular, the Scottish game and it was an absolute pleasure writing something that will hopefully bring enjoyment to a wide audience.

Special shout out to David Scott for sharing his wisdom on a number of topics and also to Roger McStravick, whom I bumped into on a street in St Andrews just before this book was published and, as always, oozed passion for the place.

Last but not least, thanks to my wife, Carol, for her unwavering support as I set our alarm even earlier than normal so that I could do my day job for *Scotsman* before turning my attention to writing this book.

Also to our oldest daughter, Amy, who is a true bookworm, for being a valuable pair of eyes as I worked through the chapters and to her sister, Katie, as well for her equally-important words of encouragement.

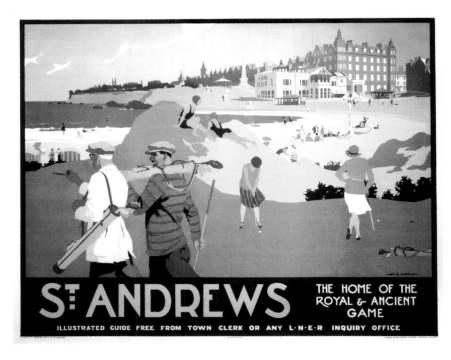

London and North Eastern Railway, St. Andrews, The Home of the Royal and Ancient Game, by Henry Gawthorn, about 1927. LNER

Printed by Waterlow and Sons Limited. Format: quad royal. Dimensions: 40 x 50 inches, 1016 x 1270 mm.

IMAGE CREDITS

Photography courtesy of:

Action Plus Sports Images/Alamy Stock
  Photo   36, 221

Alastair Chalmers   6

ALIKI SAPOUNTZI/aliki image library/Alamy
  Stock Photo   156

Alister Firth/Alamy Stock Photo   5

Allan Wright/Alamy Stock Photo   238

Allstar Picture Library Ltd/Alamy Stock
  Photo   11, 37, 200

Andrew Thomson/Comrie Golf Club   79, 123,
  138

Arterra Picture Library/Alamy Stock
  Photo   223

Associated Press/Alamy Stock Photo   34,
  92, 101, 105, 107, 111, 226, 228, 230

Brian Clark   184

Brian Morgan/Alamy Stock Photo   188

Cabot Highlands   133

Callander Golf Club   19

Carnoustie Golf Links   196, 210

CDG/Alamy Stock Photo   41

Charles Urquhart   7, 6

Christopher Ames/Alamy Stock Photo   10

Darren Chisholm   98

Darren Kirk/Alamy Stock Photo   26, 2119

David Burgon for Eyemouth Golf Club   86,
  87

David Hamilton   49

David Scott   38, 39, 189

Dunbar Golf Club   vi, 97, 130

Dundonald Links   136

Euan Cherry/Alamy Stock Photo   8

Findlay/Alamy Stock Photo   61, 171

Gleneagles   119

GolfClubs4Cash Ltd   160

Hans Linden/Alamy Stock Photo   242

Iain Carrie/Callander Golf Club   21, 218

Iain Masterton/Alamy Stock Photo   57, 77,
  125, 126, 177, 236

Iain Sarjeant/Alamy Stock Photo   154

Ian Paterson/Alamy Stock Photo   209

Ian Rutherford/Alamy Stock Photo   89

Ingolf Pompe 27/Alamy Stock Photo   235

Insidefoto di andrea staccioli/Alamy Stock
  Photo   112

Jacob Sjoman   82

James Knowler/Getty Images   106

Jim McKenzie   208

John Davidson Photos/Alamy Stock
  Photo   3